Big in Business

Dr. Ivan Misner
Beth Misner

Norm Dominguez

Hsu, Hung

Huang, Hsing-Hui

Givers Gain®

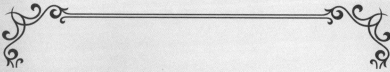

Special Dedication to:

Dr. Ivan Misner and Beth Misner

Mr. Norm Dominguez

Andrew Hall and Ji-Hong Hall

For Changing the Way the World

Does Business®

Table of Contents

Recommendation

Speacial Contents

Chapter Ⅰ. Mindset

Chapter Ⅱ. Creating an Effective Network

Chapter Ⅲ. Building Productive Relationship

Chapter Ⅳ. Effective Marketing Strategies

Chapter Ⅴ. Referral Strategy

Chapter Ⅵ. Integrating into Life

Chapter Ⅶ. 42 Taiwanese noble entrepreneurs' inspiring stories

Chapter Ⅷ. Glossary

Knowledge brings inspiration. Knowledge brings wealth.

Chung-Shu WU President of CIER

President of CIER (Chung-Hua Institution for Economic Research)
Researcher of IEAS (Institute of Economics, Academia Sinica)
Adjunct Professor, Department of Economics, National Taiwan University
President (Chairman/ Director) of TEA
(Taiwan Economic Association)
President (Chairman/ Director) of CAFES
(Chung-Hua Association for Financial and Economic Strategies)

Chung-Hua Institution for Economic Research has been founded for 30 years. It has played a critical part in decision making about the economic directions of Taiwan. The CIER leading by Chung-Shu WU does not trail the government's footsteps. President Chung-Shu WU spontaneously offers suitable proposals in response to the situation of the world. During Chung-Shu's time as the president, the "green concept" and "financial industry" are the two priority research projects for we consider the developments of these two industries are extremely important.

Under the introduction of the secretary-general of TAPAFPP (Taiwan Asia Pacific Association of Financial Planning Professionalism) Simon Liu, Chung-Shu met the two authors of this book. After the thorough study of each chapter. I could feel the vitality of the commerce in Taiwan. The focus of this book differed from my researches before. It describes a more in-depth of noble entrepreneurs in all walks of lives. Didn't all the great occurrences start from the trivial details? If you have seriously observed the developments of the economics of Taiwan. I am used to researching the monetary economics, the international finance and economic forecasts from broader perspectives. On the contrary, the touching stories of unimportant people (small potatoes/nobody) indicate the explosive power and the parts these general noble entrepreneurs contribute to the economic growth of Taiwan.

The green industry is the inevitable trend after the global warming and there are more and more entrepreneurs in Taiwan focusing on this direction. This is very encouraging wishes and it matched with the mission of this book which is to bring to world's attention to the MIT products and services provide by the noble entrepreneurs in Taiwan.

Hsu, Hung's vision is to promote the essential oil made in Taiwan to become a world known brand. Language is the basic tool for expanding your industries. If students or industries in Taiwan forget to cultivate their English ability then it would only be a slogan to claim that we have the international vision of the world.

The author of English version had a mission to use her advantage of language to gain the heart of the people in the world with the culture charm of Chinese with such ambition. We therefore gave birth to this inspiring tool book.

In this book, we can continue to see the perseverance and creativity of Taiwanese. Even with all the disadvantage conditions we insist on searching for the turning over opportunities. Just as it is described in the song "Embrace", we can see the toughness of striving for success, the passion burned with life. It is very inspiring. What Chung-Shu has been involved in more rational research because you don't usually find emotion in economics? This book made Chung-Shu begin to think about the sensibility in economics.

Money is a trading tool. A tool for storing value and book keeping. The spirit and method used in this book is the transactions for completing contracts.

The desire of letting Taiwan be seen by the world is the love to our motherland. They try to build the trust internationally. It is the fixative of international finance.

You need to have accurate statistics and research data to be able to predict the economic. Chung-Shu cannot analyze the selling of this book with scientific research. However I can boldly predict the popularity of this book will wave miraculous leap for business in Taiwan.

As an important national professional, I have to be cautious about what I say and how I behavior. But I would like to enthusiastically recommend this book. I sincerely hope that every Taiwanese can read it carefully.

Chung-Shu Wu 05.04 2015

Rekindle the competitive power of Taiwan.

Chien-Fu Lin President of TIER

President of TIER (Taiwan Institution of Economic Research)
Professor, Department of Economics,National Taiwan University

Over the years of struggling in the field of economics, the practical education for economic development has always been the direction of my efforts. And the competitiveness of Taiwan is my passion never dies out.

The vital of enterprise lies in talent employees and the spirit of Taiwan lies in its people. To strengthen the competitiveness power of Taiwan, the 23 million Taiwanese should take up the responsibility.

Production, manufacturing, quality control, planning, marketing, language, trading and management are indispensable links in operating businesses. We must know exactly what is the direction of our effort to achieve multiplier effects. With words and no action, we can't escalate our economy. Without integrating systems and plans, the high performance of economy can't reach the setting goal.

A great economy is neither gifts from heaven nor stocks or lotteries we buy and pray for it to win. It is the combat power we accumulate step by step. This is a world full with surprises. The reason why there is surprise is because not everything follows its fixed tracks. We can always find something new. Disasters and luck are what's new in life and as well as economics.

We can't either dream about finding rich oil field along the coast of Hualien or rediscovered gold mine in the mountains of Jinguashi. We can't wake up in the morning and find diamonds cover our land. These can't be called "news". They only happen in our dreams.

However, I found something new after reading this book. Every story in this book is full of inspiration. All the characters carry the potential for creating miracles.

Marketing is the accelerator for economic. Cultural creations are the beautiful packaging for economy. I wouldn't have discovered all the hopes behinds the small industries in Taiwan if I haven't read this book.

These two authors cooperate in these two bilingual books with dream to coherent the positive energy in the industries in Taiwan. To make Taiwan be seen, these behaviors are the same as those athletes who compete in international games carrying our national flag. These books could have more unpredictable influences because they are published in both paper and electronic. The power of internet is far-reaching.

Team based word of mouth marketing seems to be a successful replication model which is a new mechanism has not yet been carried forward in the history of marketing. If the government can lead this mode of operation, the competitiveness of Taiwan will double instantly. We can create a super enterprise group.

I was moved and excited. I can't help but give a warm applause to the authors. I also have this deep expectation for every business people in Taiwan to become noble entrepreneurs. We cooperate and join forces for Taiwan.

This is a good book. A good book that rekindle the competitiveness of Taiwan.

Chien-Fu Lin 05.04 2015

Taking ten years to sharpen a sword (Chinese words) Persistence is the key to success!

Kuo-Chien Yu Professor

Present
Vice President of JANFUSUN FANCYWORLD CORP.
Chair Professor, Graduate Program of Sustainable Tourism and Recreation Management, National Taichung University of Education
Adjunct Professor, Department of Tourism Management, Nanhua University

Experience
Senior Edition Director, Planner, Producer of TAIWAN TELEVISION CULTURAL ENTERPRISE LTD.
President for Program of Cheng Sheng Broadcasting Corp.
Adjunct Professor, Graduate Institute of Travel and Tourism Management, National Kaohsiung University of Hospitality and Tourism
Adjunct Professor, Executive Master of Business Administration, National Chiayi University

Award
National Manager Excellence Award 2000

Every time I read a new book, I try to study the struggle of the author at the same time. I would like to read behind and know the author's thoughts and attitude of life. Before I recommend this book, I would like to introduce the author first.

The author's father is a well-known fortune teller who is a close friend of mine for more than half century. I have been through a long tough journey in live together. I was older. He respected me as elder brother and I take care of his family including his spouse and his 3 children. All his children have his work hard spirit like Forrest Gump. They work hard hand in hand from scrap to abundant today.

Hsu, Hung is his eldest son and I know he will be "somebody" ever since he was little. He is talented and extremely intelligent. When he was in his graduate school, I found him has the "Four basic skills young adults have" as the Japanese writer Shinji Yamamoto described. There are: "The ability to work hard", "The ability to learn", "The ability to accept" and most of all "The ability to challenge". He was longing for my career devoting in creation and innovation. I spend my whole life exceeding fixed thoughts and searching ways to set my own irreplaceable role in business. I had forgotten to tell him that doing what I do is well regarded in front of people glanced but had been through the hardship of life behind people.

I know Hsu, Hung well. He is always eager to prove himself.

He started to drive himself as hard as an ironman even before he graduated from graduate school. He relied on his own ability and introduced himself to all kinds of projects like innovation, activity designing, promotion etc. he was managed to write, to publish and gave speeches at the same time. He used his passion and positive attitude to create his own future.

I admire this outstanding junior. The past decades he has used his brain, mouth, hands and legs with his faith. There was nothing he can't accomplish. He never let any opportunities of creating the value of his personal brand slip away.

This is the book he put all his wisdom he accumulated through life. To have a place in the field of creation, you need at least 10 years to come up with the two value systems the author holds. One is his unlimited creation. He can invent any kind of products from sketch and create irreplaceable unique value. The other is his innovation as an entrepreneur to integrate and achieve multiple effects. According to these two points, it is not difficult to tell the special content of this book. It describes 42 true stories of how these elites strive for their success with 40 intellectual and practical knowledge gained articles and put them together. It is erudite and multi-talented. The distinguishing features of this book is the "perspective of a bird" to observe the horizon of the world and the "vision of a worm" to evaluate the details cautiously. He also uses his culture to refute the preclude injustice bureaucratic habits and hereditary disorder.

The most admirable thing is the author introspects while writing and searching the inner truth and justice. At the same time he tries to deliver the moral and ethic of human beings.

In short this book is rigorous yet lively, elegant yet imaginative. It is highly recommended to give your friend one and keep one for yourself. Put it next to tour bed, read one or two chapters before going to bed. Cleaning your soul and enhance your wisdom. It would be a wonderful deed that everyone should have this book. The truth and justice is our eternal life guiding stars.

It is worthy for more praising.

Kuo-Chien Yu 05.16 2015

Big in Business

Bing-Yuan Hsiung Professor

Present
Professor, Department of Economics, National Taiwan University
Y. C. Chair Professor of Zhejiang University
Visiting Professor, City University of Hong Kong
Adjunct Professor of Xi'an Jiaotong University
Adjunct Professor of Henan Normal University

For a number of days, I have been observed my behaviors and introspected my own thoughts. I use my economic perspective to view the world and judge the conditions of economics in daily lives. These thinking patterns enable me the depth and width in vision.

I used the physical education teacher as metaphor for my job. I am the teacher who teaches how to exercise our brain. I always think it is so much worse not to exercise your brain. Therefore, the daily brain gymnastics is my requirements for my students and myself.

Everyone holds his own way in measurement. Different thoughts bring about different results. It is not hard to tell the delicacy of the two authors' philosophy. They expect themselves to use all kinds of examples in Chinese culture to express the good and honest sides of business people. And they cooperate with other in order to achieve greater goals. Hsu, Hung and Hsing-Hui gathered 42 experts from different industries and described their hard work on the way to success. They also provide unlimited potential in connecting each other. They have formed an invincible team.

I studied military strategy and tactics and explore the art of business. Because they are the variable factors in economy. I especially enjoy the chapters discussing about word of mouth referral marketing. They gave me a lot of inspiration.

They are not ordinary marketing strategy and tactics if we use them well and promote the concept of group referrals among different industries. It could be another new wave of economic legend. We need this positive thinking and energy for this economic recession. Economy and trends are the creation of mankind. We should say no to recession. Each noble entrepreneur is determined for success. They created their own bright destinies. They not only benefit themselves but also contribute the world. I found all their devotion to the love of Taiwan.

I am moved therefore I share. I support therefore I recommend.

This book is like a beacon. The beacon that lights up the hope for economics breakthrough. And the beacon that shows the ideal purpose of lives.

I want to say: We appreciate your devotion. I hope that your influence and spirit as noble entrepreneurs will spread to each corner in Taiwan.

Big in Business! I like it!

Bing-Yuan Hsiung 05.04 2015

The Soul of the Success

Kan-Nan Chen Professor

Present
Professor, Department of Chemical and Material Engineering, Tamkang University

Experience
Academic Vice President of Tamkang University
Dean, College of Science, Tamkang University
Chairman, Department of Chemistry, Tamkang University
Chief Officer, Office of Research and Development, Tamkang University
Professor, Department of Chemistry, Tamkang University

This is another heart moving moment that one of my favorite students has another book to publish. What matters is, this one is a bilingual book for global reading.

In the past, my students and I have so many chemistry and material related theses published in overseas professional periodicals, in English of course, for which is still the most common language in use worldwide. Therefore, Hsu, Hung and Hsing-Hui Huang creatively wrote a book about 42 entrepreneurs' great stories; together they verified again their visions.

I used to like to say Hsu, Hung ignores his own professional work because he has good fundamental knowledge of chemistry and material but has not developed on the path of research and study. Instead, he went for the commercials. Nevertheless, based on his literal and eloquent talents, it truly is a pity to keep him in the industrial field. So I was optimistic about his choice of future. From a tutoring teacher, pharmaceutical factory trainer, corporate consultant and general manager, to even CEO, every time I met Hsu, Hung he gave me nonstop surprises. Being able to educate the talented people is the desire of all teachers in the world.

And then Hsu, Hung started his own business from importing and operating brands, setting up factory, essence oil factory, building up the glory of MIT (Made in Taiwan). That is when Hsu, Hung returned to his professional business. At the moment he has known how to put the world trend and market demand into the creation of the product research. Me as a teacher is fortunate to see it happen.

Hsu, Hung in college was trained with variety of physics and chemistry during the experiments in the lab. He smoothly combined experimental data with industrial values thus today his life career as beauty care by making natural essence oil. This is how he integrates what he learns into business.

From reading this book it is not difficult to see Hsu, Hung's power of integration. He's able to make every entrepreneur's story so vivid, even the main role of each story is touched. Most moving is, Hsu, Hung never forgets he is a Taiwanese even he has good progress made in foreign countries. If all Taiwanese are like him having such faith and action, wishing to be able to make a difference for Taiwan, it will be the most honorable country in the world.

The flattery for my own student seems so biased. However I have to praise for this book's great practical values.

If learning is for feeding a mouth, you will lack motivation.

If a diploma is for bluffing, it will soon be unmasked.

This book tells you what it is for learning and gaining a diploma.

The link of academy and industry is an extension that I've never given up. Research is for development, and for development you must research. The two can never be separated. No matter academically or industrially, this book is worth reading by every and each team member of your business.

Work hard and work smart! This is my line! Hsu, Hung realized my words in life that I'm so moved. I recommend this book which has the most energy in the world, for in this book I found the element that cannot be found in periodictableoftheelements, and that is the soul of the success.

Kan-Nan Chen 05.04 2015

Scale and Attitude

Po-Hsun Hsiao, Associate Professor

General Manager of JANFUSUN FANCYWORLD CORP.
(1987-2009)
Ph.D. of Business Management, National Yunlin University of
Science and Technology
Associate Professor, National Taiwan University of Sport

Congratulations to Hsu, Hung of H2, MIT (Made in Taiwan). After the achievement of the four books—Accomplishment in Split Second, Beauty Care in Split Second, Marketing in Split Second, Leading in Split Second—Hsu, Hung continues to spread the charm as a professional essential oil master publish The Taste of Huge Business, which sharing the recent 10 years practice experience as Hsu, Hung having been corporate advisor, consultant in chief, general manager to innovate and startup. With a faith of true, kind, and beauty, he consistently carries out a business citizen's responsibilities while humbly taking in all words and spreading out goodwill of health and happiness.

Nowadays is the age of experiencing economy. In "Big in

Business" Hsu, Hung's point of view grasps what customers genuinely desire is the "reality, which has taken place of quality of the products and become the main standard for people to consume. Moreover, the essential oil business Hsu, Hung and his team created shows the "reality" of natural elements, returning the products to the "lifestyle" that matters. To create one's own lifestyle and motto is pursued by creators and housekeepers of aesthetics who are thirsty to experience reality.

Hsu, Hung especially has a great insight of the market, where he learns from humbly. He not only satisfies consumption demand, but innovates it in order to achieve the Taste of Huge Business with a grateful mind.

The 42 poetries written with lives are 42 stories of 42 great businessmen gathered by the Taste of Huge Business. Every and each businessman's fighting battles and positive energy enable us to see their scales and attitudes toward facing difficulties in life. There is no reason for us to give up ourselves with such encouragement.

For Hsu, Hung's big heart he can contain all matters worldly; and his humbleness allows him to accept all the goods as well. His heart has no attachment so it is free. The Taste of Huge Business is sweet. Let's appreciate the taste.

Po-Hsun Hsiao 05.16 2015

Glorifying Taiwan starts by Business Pioneers

Long Ou-Yang Taipei City Councilor

Life is like a theater, and vice versa.

Having been an actor makes me feel deeply that no matter what roles you are playing in your own life, you have to be that character. We can only reach such level by interpreting every role with our own lives.

I am sincerely thankful to my electors for their affirmation and support. Electors are like audience. If my performance is below expectation, before my due schedule I'd be gone without a future to looking forward. Therefore, every single say as a voice of our people I am careful and fully focused.

After a long talk with two writers and reading the book, I was so moved. If Taiwan's political parties see each other without stereotype nor bear no past burden, and when it comes to people's affairs, the administration would attend on executing good policies, and councilors would speak up for the mass and oversee every details of the execution. With this strong cooperation Taiwan must be a great country.

Small doesn't mean weak, and weak doesn't mean none, and none doesn't mean there'll be no more.

If we can put our strength together and make it small but beautiful and powerful, the long lost glory can shine once again. We can no longer congregate just by tragic emotions, nor can we just live in our own bubbles. And we can never ever lose track with the international by contenting with what we have created in the past decades.

This is the first book written in Chinese and synchronously translated in English and published worldwide. The bilingual book globalization in which Ou-Yang is honored by writing a foreword. The author said Ou-Yang in their eye is not only a political figure, but a friend of Taiwan who means what he says and does what he promises. Just at the moment he's playing a role of Taipei City Councilor.

Taiwan is a wonderful land. The people living in here are a kind and good crowd. However when it arrives 21st century, we have seemed lack of team work force power but only weakening and vilifying one another.

Politics is the foundation of stabilization and prosper. Business is the seed of fire to thrive. There are so many stories of huge businesses in Taiwan, not just paparazzi bad news from the media covers.

Taiwan needs the author's encouraging words for tremendous stories as such in the book. The 42 noble entrepreneurs are not celebrities however they make their own way step by step responsibly, fighting for Taiwan's future.

Such sentiment for a country is greatness. Huge business fits the character. The author divides businessmen into huge, small, none, and wicked. So does Ou-Yang looking at political figures.

Wicked are known as politicians. None has only ideas and thoughts without putting a hand in anything. Small only cares about votes and continuing in office. Huge needs to take care of interests of people and society. The meanings both happen to hold the similar view.

I set an expectation for myself, that when I play a role of a civilian I can still goal at huge politics, in order to serve my country and people. Thus hereby I recommend this book with sense and sensibility.

To read a book is profitable, especially this one. To seek interests for my people, especially in a huge way.

Glorifying Taiwan starts by Business Pioneers

Long Ou-Yang 05.10 2015

She Tries Harder

James Yu CEO of HoldFuture

Hsing-Hui Huang-I finally have an opportunity to help you. I am more than willing to use my hard-won reputation to testify for you. Besides our priceless friendship, you are worthy of my true-hearted recommendation.

It is my honor to do so. I remember the first time I met Hsing-Hui. She welcomed me happily and treated me with the best quality tea and endless laughter like a carefree angel. It was not until we had known each other for some time that I learned that it was the toughest period of her life. She was going through a period of betrayal and had almost nothing left. She had just had two major surgeries and her business was like a small boat being tossed about by the wind and rain. She was penniless.

Can you image living in such a terrible condition? However, I never heard any complaints or outpourings of her suffering. She just smiled and laughed at her own misery. One time she found a ten dollar coin on the ground. She cheerfully picked it up and exclaimed,

"Wow! My savings have risen ten times. I am so lucky." She chose to stay optimistic and confronted the challenges life had given her.

I am not sure what kind of lessons God wanted her to learn. What I can be sure is that she is now so much different after all these years. During those difficult times, she never gave up learning. She spent every penny she could gather on improving herself. She is creating value to her life and bringing inspiration to others.

From a societal standpoint, we cannot say she is "successful" because she doesn't have millions in her bank account and hasn't become extremely famous-yet. However, this "not successful yet" woman has never surrendered to destiny. She always laughs out loud. She firmly believes in helping others to become successful first. She is extraordinarily wealthy in her social capital account. She is actually on her way to success and those experiences in her life are precious assets on her track.

Life will find its way. The life for Hsing-Hui is no exception, hers just seems more circuitous. I don't know where God is leading her, but I am sure that He is waiting for her, ready to give back every reward she deserves. After having accomplished her tasks, having been through thick and thin in life, I can guarantee that the problems and challenges she has confronted will become a priceless lesson.

Her speed of personal growth over the past two years has exceeded everyone's expectations. She is a completely different person; she she card no longer be defined by her past failures. She dug herself out of the valley. She told me she was about to publish a book, that she wanted to share the experiences and trials of her tour in finding a purpose in life. I am so happy for her. This book will be a gift for so many people. Pick up the book and read it, you will know why I say so.

Hsing-Hui has taught English all her life. Now she is using her talent to allow more Westerners to understand the things of Eastern Philosophy. Hsing-Hui has walked her own path. She has lived by her own values. She has been on the way for so long, I believe this is finally the beginning of her good fortune. Every word in this book contains tremendous meaning from the lives of those whose stories are told in the book. It is a wonderful gift to readers lucky enough to pick up the book and read it. I sincerely hope that you can receive the heart that Hsing-Hui wants to present.

Everywhere we hear stories about dreams, mediocre family lives and the contradictions in society with reality. All these many elements connect our splendid lives. We strive hard to survive. The true stories from the Taiwanese in this book represent the fortitudinous spirit of the Taiwanese people. It is an epitome of Eastern cultural values.

The Hsing-Hui I know is a person who never gives up in giving abundant and valuable exchange. She truly believes one's life must matter. She keeps on giving and walks the talk of helping others. Throughout this book, she has combined her thoughts, and if any story has touched your heart, it is the result of her efforts.

Through her selfless giving, Hsing-Hui has given spirit to this book. Her sincerity helps to rekindle passion and persistence in our lives.

Hsing-Hui, you are the friend whom I can trust and rely on. It's wonderful to have you. Your existence makes the world a better place.

I hope you can bring this feeling into all our lives and help us to change ourselves and bring more meaning into our society.

James Yu 06.04 2015

Preface

This preface was co-written by Hsu, Hung and Hsing-Hui Huang with the most grateful thanks about this creation book.

The initial for Hsu, Hung is H2 and the initial for Hsing-Hui Huang is H3. Therefore the combination for these two authors is H5 and is the best ever (Number 1). We called ourselves H5N1. We are not an influenza virus. However, we want to have fast and far-reaching influence and leave a remarkable legend. The birth of this book is a miracle meant to be. We appreciate the 42 participants for their trust and their encouraging stories in striving for greater meanings for success and life. We are certain about the mission of these two books. And we are also thankful to the seven great recommenders. Their recognition and encouragement inspire us to carry out our aspiration.

We went through great assistance. We also encountered various obstacles and interference. All these challenges made the outcome more valuables. We tore in writing the stories and we sweated at the accumulation of "Art of war" for business. This book was the splendid works with sweat and tears.

The training for organizations and not telling or doing without knowing the "why" and this book provides the materials and stories for trainings. The spirit of organization marketing, the cooperation and collaboration in networking platform can be found here. Thus, this is the coaching manual, the commercial art of war book and it is also the guidebook for business people in networking marketing.

The 42 amazing stories of noble entrepreneurs we describe are the combination of specialization and cooperation. These are not the advertisements in newspaper or magazines. They are the presentation of true life stories. All these people who have been reported are still working really hard to make differences in the world from Taiwan.

Thus, this is a motivational book with role models to inspire the youth to strive for success. It's the incisive reference for people who dare to challenge.

It is also a book to encourage those helpless and unaided. After we finish reading all the stories we would have no more excuses for not being able to become successful.

This is the first book in the history of book publishing in Taiwan that is published simultaneously in both Chinese and English. It's the Taiwanese style of touching and moving. We would love the spirit and wonder of the noble entrepreneurs from Taiwan to be seen in the whole world.

We are proud to be Taiwanese and expect to influence more people with our outcome. We dedicate this book to our motherland Taiwan and all the Taiwanese that we've grown up with.

We love Taiwan because we come from Taiwan.

Special Content

Biography
Norm Dominguez

Norm Dominguez is the former CEO of BNI® (Business Network International), which was founded in 1985. The organization has over 6,200 chapters throughout every populated continent of the world. Last year alone, BNI® generated 6.9 million referrals resulting in $3.1 billion dollars worth of business for its members.

Mr. Dominguez is a graduate of The University of Colorado. He has been associated with BNI® since 1987. In addition to being CEO, he oversees his BNI® franchises in Arizona. He is a strong supporter of the BNI® Charitable Foundation which aids in both children and educational programs. He serves on the Board of Directors for the Le Roy Haynes Center in La Verne, CA. He has served as Chairman of the BNI® Franchise Advisory Board and has been a BNI® District Director for the Rocky Mountain/Southwest Regions. He is a member of the Founders Circle, which he chairs along with Dr. Ivan Misner®, Founder&Chief Visionary Officerof BNI®. He is a contributing author in the New York Times bestseller Masters of Networking.

EVERYDAY MATTERS

By Norm Dominguez

What you did yesterday can very well effect today and what you do today may very well have an impact on tomorrow! Thus **EVERYDAY MATTERS** regardless. I remember reading the following thought from Confucius, "Where-so-ever you go, go with all your heart". Every morning I find myself expressing gratitude, knowing that there will be a plethora of blessings and happy thoughts ahead for each of us.

A few years ago I was thinking about why does everyday matter? Five words quickly came to mind. They were **IMAGINATION, FREEDOM, TRUST, HOPE AND ATTITUDE,** with each having a meaningful impact.

IMAGINATION-when I was quite young my parents moved to Southern California. Soon thereafter, they took my brothers and I to the 'happiest place on earth' Disneyland where we got to meet

Mickey, Minnie, Goofy and many of the other Disney characters. We were introduced to the magic of Walt Disney. In my mind, Disney demonstrated the glory of imagination. He gave us a place that transferred ideas into something real.

Decades later, with our children and grandchildren, my wife and I enjoy the Disney adventure. Through the cast members at Disney, we enjoy the work of Imaginers at the parks, in the movies, with the games and toys that are created and memories that each experience imprints in our minds. There is nothing like imagination.

FREEDOM- a word too often taken for granted. My life has given me a great appreciation of freedom having been many places in the United States and around the world where it is not given the respect or honor deserved. **There is no greater gift than knowing that rights and thoughts are the highest priority.**

There are many examples to draw from. Since the early 2000's countries around the world have faced terrorist attacks. In every case the people have risen to defend their freedom. It is more than a point of pride. It is a commitment to beliefs. Remember the September 11 attack in the United States when there were numerous attacks. Nations have come together to establish a war on terrorism. This continues to create a united bond around the world in defense of freedom.

During the last century, individuals like Winston Churchill,

Mother Teresa, Martin Luther King Jr, Nelson Mandela and many others have defended the importance of freedom. They have been an inspiration to billions of people. Freedom sets a positive course for everyday motivation.

TRUST-within the life picture there is a strong belief that trust is the single most important factor in building personal and professional relationships. I have been a part of the world's largest referral marketing company (BNI®) for nearly three decades and a foundational component of the organization is directly related to trust. Warren Bennis and Burt Nanus, noted leadership experts, call trust **"the glue that binds followers and leaders together"**, which leads to putting accountability and reliability at the forefront of all of our actions.

I'm reminded of the 'good old fashioned handshake' that delivers a message of agreement. Every day we find ourselves in a position of doing something as simple as relaying a request or as complex as completing an assignment, which turns out to be an action of trust. **The key is to make sure we respect the importance of being trustworthy.** It is one of our most valuable assets!

HOPE-this is the eternal glow that carries us into the future. It is the optimistic side of our lives. My favorite quote comes from **Churchill, "Never, never, never give up".** I have a custom license plate frame on my car that carries his message. I see and read it daily. His spirit resonates clearly as he kept people engaged in a path to retain freedom globally during World War II. We should have an obligation of hope deeply lodged in our beliefs that allows us to prosper.

In 2004 I had a stroke without any warning. My recovery took months. For the better part of two years I feared going to sleep at night wondering if I'd wake up the next morning. Family, friends and hope got me through this period. This was a warning signal that will always be with me. I am forever grateful to have been surrounded by those that care. **I praise the glory that comes from hope.**

ATTITUDE-it comes from within. It can be one's greatest asset or liability. Every morning I greet the day with being thankful there is NO dirt on my face and being able to GIVE the entire day my best shot. My first encounter with attitude was the 'ole on the shoulder spirit that did not leave a favorable impression', and it was displayed in a cocky way. This was not good. Over time I came to recognize the importance of a positive mindset that translated into always thinking that life is remarkable (naturally the upside of remarkable☺)

It has turned into a journey approaching three decades of being surrounded by attitudinal excellence. There are no limits, only opportunities of success.

Having this mindset makes things possible . . . not easy. There will be obstacles; they become reality checks as one climbs the ladder of happiness and positivity. Yes, attitude is everything!

AND NOW WHAT HAPPENS?

As I was looking at the words of **EVERYDAY MATTERS** with some curiosity, I discovered that a new acronym could be created from the first letter of each word. **The acronym is F.A.I.T.H. It spells an old word 'faith' with very deep roots. Now it is given a new look without changing the joy and inspiration that has delivered an important meaning to billions of people for a long, long time.**

It is my wish, that each of us can take the new look and blend it with the old meaning, thus adopting a simple approach to make EVERY DAY MATTER.

Don't Let your Past Failure Define your Future

By Hsing-Hui Huang

Sometimes we hesitate and cannot make up our mind because we are hindered by our past failures. We are afraid to make the wrong decisions and get hurt or blamed. We tend to avoid being the cause of making the wrong choices.

In our dilemma we sometimes need advice from a consultant or mentor. It is very critical who we ask for our suggestions.

If we have a great investment opportunity from a business partner who has been extremely successful in real estate, such as a proposal to cooperate with him and guaranteeing that we can develop our fortune, we might be afraid and excited at the same time. We are excited for the opportunity of a lifetime; we are scared because we have heard so many bad stories about failures in real estate.

If we consult this proposal with our friend whose average salary is US$1000 a month. What would his suggestion be?

Never ask a bicycle rider about their experiences in driving a Ferrari.

Never ask a farmer about how to fly a fighter aircraft.

It would be like asking me a Calculus question. What I am good at is English, not Math.

To understand a profession in a field there are only two choices.

Either we try it ourselves or we seek advices from those who are successful and have professional expertise in the field.

Don't spend our energy in thinking and planning and then be hindered by our fear.

When I was writing this book I really wished I could have Norm Dominguez, the Vice Chair Emeritus of BNI® to write the preface for us.

I translated for Norm in his speech at the 2013 BNI® Taiwan Convention and we had a great time working together. Later that year at the BNI® International Convention, Norm brought me up on the stage to demonstrate the meaning of "Trust". We built our credibility there.

Norm is a leader that we really look up to. He has devoted most of his life to the world's largest referral marketing company, BIN® and he walks the talk in building personal and professional relationships. We admire him so much. However I was stopped by my own fear of failure, the **imaginary rejection** hindered me from asking.

What encouraged me was a video by Dr. Ivan Misner®, the Founder and Chief Visionary Officer for BNI®, the world's largest business networking organization, my other role model. The video was entitled" How to Combat the Fear of Failure. I was really surprised that Dr. Ivan Misner® has had a business that failed too.

He mentioned that we can't define ourselves by our failures in life and shared his experiences in book publishing and the solution he used to combat his fear of failure. (You have to watch the video yourselves. I now watch it every time I worry about failure.)

It inspired me and I was able to gather my courage to write Mr. Norm Dominguez an email and invited him to write the preface for our book. Norm replied and he gave more than was expected. Not only did he agree but he wrote this enlightening article for all readers. It is such a beautiful story.

First of all, **I know whom to consult** when I face challenges or have doubts in life! (The answer is very obvious!!)

Second of all, **I know to take action.**

However, the most critical factor is that Norm put the culture of "Givers Gain®" into practice.

Thank you Dr. Misner and Mr Dominguez for the positive influence and for what you've done for us.

Biography
Ivan Misner®, Ph.D.

Dr. Ivan Misner® is the Founder and Chief Visionary Officer of BNI®, the world's largest business networking organization. Founded in 1985 the organization now has over 7,100 chapters throughout every populated continent of the world. Last year alone, BNI® generated 6.6 million referrals resulting in $8.6 billion dollars' worth of business for its members. Dr. Misner's Ph.D. is from the University of Southern California. He is a New York Times Bestselling author who has written 20 books. He is also a columnist for Entrepreneur.com and Fox Business News and has taught business management at several universities throughout the United States. In addition, he is the Senior Partner for the Referral Institute-a referral training company with trainers around the world. Called the "Father of Modern Networking" by CNN and one off the "Top Networking Experts to Watch" by Forbes, Dr. Misner is considered to be one of the world's leading experts on business networking and has been a keynote speaker for major corporations and associations throughout the world. He has been featured in the L.A. Times, Wall Street Journal, and New York. Times, as well as numerous TV and radio shows including CNN, the BBC and The Today Show on NBC. Dr. Misner is on the Board of Trustees for the University of LaVerne. He is also the Co-Founder of the BNI® Charitable Foundation and was recently named "Humanitarian of the Year" by the Red Cross. He and his wife, Elisabeth, are now "empty nesters" with three adult children... Oh, and in his spare time he is also an amateur magician and a black belt in karate.

OMG, I'm an Introvert!?

By Dr. Ivan Misner®

OK, if you don't know what "OMG" means, ask a teenager (that's how I learned what it meant). Now let's talk about the introvert thing.

My wife and I were having a relaxing dinner one night recently. We were sitting around the kitchen table talking when I made some off-handed comment about being an extrovert (it fit into the context of the conversation). She looked over at me and said, "Uhh, honey, I hate to break it to you, but you're an introvert." I smiled and said, "Yeah, sure, I'm an introvert (insert laugh track here)." She then looked at me quite earnestly and said, "No, really you're an introvert." I protested strongly. I said, "Come on, I'm a public speaker and founder of the world's largest networking organization–I'm not an introvert! I can't be. I mean, you're joking, right?" She absolutely insisted that I was an introvert and proceeded to share with me all the ways that I have introverted tendencies. Well, I have to admit I was taken back by this. All the examples she gave were true, but I still couldn't believe I am an introvert. On the other hand, we've been married for 20 years. I mean, there's a chance she might actually know me pretty well.

So off I went the next day to do some research. I did an internet search and found a test that tells you whether you are an introvert or extrovert. Was I in for a shock. The test said that I was a "situational extrovert!" It explained that I was something of a loner who was reserved around strangers but very outgoing in the right context. It was at that moment that I said, "OMG, I'm an introvert!?"

In the haze of my surprise, some very important things came into clarity for me. It struck me why I started the BNI® networking organization more than two decades ago. I was naturally uncomfortable meeting new people. This approach created a "system" that enabled me to meet people in an organized, structured, networking environment that did not require that I actually "talk to strangers." OMG, I'm an introvert!

When I visit regions of BNI®, I ask my director to have someone walk me around and introduce me to visitors and members so that I can connect with as many people as possible. But in reality, it's because I'm uncomfortable walking around introducing myself alone. OMG, I'm an introvert!

I realized that the whole notion of "acting like the host, not the guest" and volunteering to be the ambassador at a chamber event or the visitor host at a BNI® group were all the ways I used to move around more comfortably at networking events, not just ways that I recommended for those poor introverts out there to network. OMG, I am an introvert.

Who would have thought? Well, OK, besides my lovely wife. Now more than ever, I truly believe that whether you are an introvert or an extrovert, you can be good at networking. Both have strengths and weaknesses. If you can find ways to enhance your strengths and minimize your weaknesses, anyone can be a great networker.

How about you? Are you an introvert or an extrovert, and how do you use that in your networking?

Culture Eats Strategy For Breakfast

By Dr. Ivan Misner®

Strategy is often talked about in business schools, in fact it's a primary focus. Culture however, is less understood. Culture involves a variety of contributing factors including a blend of attitudes, beliefs, mission, philosophy, and momentum that help to create and sustain a successful brand. It represents the vision, norms, symbols, beliefs, behaviors, and traditions that are taught to new members of an organization. Organizational culture affects the way people within an organization interact with one another and the people they serve.

Culture is key in an organization for long-term success. It is the most important thing in an organization and it applies at all levels, from the top of the organization all the way down. Rules, regulations, and operating standards are important, of course, because you have to have systems in place to guide activities. But culture is the factor that stands above all others.

There are many factors that go into building an organizational culture. Each successful company has a different combination of factors that makes their culture successful. Here are a few that I think are particularly important.

1.Traditions

Traditions help make a company what it is. They tell the world who they are as an organization. One way for an organization to maintain and develop its organizational culture and ethos is to introduce and celebrate a variety of traditions. Disney in particular has been a master of this concept by training all new employees on the traditions of the organization. Strong traditions that are applied throughout an organization are one of the best ways to maintain a healthy organizational culture.

2.Mission

A burning mission can give laser focus to an organization. The mission statement needs to be short and memorable. Most importantly, it needs to be a rallying cry for people throughout the organization. One thing I've learned in running a business for almost thirty years is that "ignorance on fire is better than knowledge on ice." Getting employees and clients excited about the mission is critical to organizational success. If the average employee can't recite your mission-it's too long.

3.Engagement

Collaboration encourages engagement. Get all levels of an organization involved. In BNI®, the global referral network I founded almost 30 years ago, we have focused on getting a high level of engagement at all levels of the company. This engagement includes a Franchise Advisory Board made up of key franchisees to address organizational challenges, a Founder's Circle of stake holders to provide direct feedback to management about issues concerning the organization, a Board of Advisors made up exclusively of clients to ensure engagement regarding policies that effect the organization globally, an Executive Council made up of the largest seven master franchisees within the organization, as well as a number of other entities to help ensure full participation at all levels of the organization. Engagement can be messy, but when done correctly, it encourages a collaborative culture.

4.Recognition

Many years ago, Ken Blanchard got it right in The One Minute Manager. He said, "catch people doing something right" and recognize them publicly. Praise in public and re-direct in private. No truer words have ever been spoken when it comes to building a healthy organizational culture. Recognize and celebrate successes. As Blanchard says, if you can't catch people doing something right-then catch them doing something 'partially right' and recognize that.

5.Education

Immerse and engage in a culture of learning. The more a company can integrate ongoing learning into the organizational ethos, the more likely that company is to stay nimble and prepared for change.

Educating the organization regarding the culture of the company is particularly important to fuel and maintain a great culture. A great strategy keeps you in the game, however, a great culture helps you win. Especially important are the traditions and mission of the company. These things need to be part of the ongoing education of all new and existing employees.

Culture is a critical key to organizational success. It is one of the most important things in a company and it applies to all levels, from the top of the organization all the way down. The challenge with culture is that it is illusive. The best and most scalable culture is one that is managed and maintained by the majority and not by a single policing body or by management alone.

Companies that dominate an industry for a long period of time do so because of a shared vision of organizational culture that is effectively implemented throughout the company. That shared implementation of the vision is an important key to building a successful organizational culture. If all the people in an organization row in the same direction in unison, that organization can dominate any industry, in any market, against any competition, at any time.

Implementing a strong organizational strategy can be difficult however, implementing a healthy organizational culture is rare and in my opinion when all is said and done; culture, eats strategy for breakfast any day.

Biography
Beth Misner

All my life I have found creative ways to incorporate service to others into my professional life. From being a chiropractic assistant to managing special projects for my company-BNI®, and leading the prayer ministry at my church, my one question has always been, "How can I help you?" I want to know what I can do that will make things better for those whom I support and encourage.

With the amazingly wonderful, global success of BNI®, I

have found the vehicle that allows me to use my talents, abilities, education and passion to serve others globally-the BNI® Foundation. Just as my husband, BNI® Founder Dr. Ivan Misner®, and I teach business owners to harness the power of relationship marketing to grow their profits, I am teaching them now to harness the power of collaboration and noble networking to grow our youth into strong, productive and empowered citizens through our movement, Business Voices.

Business VOICES Dream Team

By Beth Misner

Recent events in Ferguson, MO, have really touched the core of my heart. Let me start with a little background.

I spent my junior high and high school years in rural East Tennessee, in Dayton. I rode the bus to high school that picked up the kids from the projects, as we called it, before it picked up me and my brother. Most of the students picked up from the projects were black students. I was one of the few white students who would sit with black students if there were a spot open on the bus. Most of my classmates stood, rather than take a seat beside one of them. You can just imagine the names I was called. I look back on my younger self and feel grateful that I was known even then for love.

This was in the late 70's/early 80's and my high school had an active student chapter of the KKK. Once a year those students would don their garb, carry hoes and shovels and march around and around the indoor quad (followed by a hundred or more other students) while the black students and the band students-that was me-were huddled, terrified.

Some weekends, when my family would drive between Dayton and

Chattanooga, the KKK would be stopping traffic in Sale Creek with out-held boots, taking donations from drivers who would roll down their windows and put cash into the boots. Our daddy told us, "Look straight ahead. Don't roll your window down." We did exactly that.

I have a heart for the emotional damage and psychological injury racism and socio-economic inequality can cause. I am very troubled by the crippling effects of racism in our country. And I feel devastated by the condition of the inner city schools-the schools that are filled with extremely economically challenged students.

As I watched the events in Ferguson, MO, recently, I saw the anguish and pain on the faces and heard the heart ache in the words of the members of this community (NOT the agitators and those who were using this time to highjack the protests for their own purposes), I found myself wanting to do something to let them know that I personally care-that BNI® personally cares. I want them to know that I heard them saying, "we need help in order that the present situation can change."

I thought about finding a school in Ferguson to which the BNI® Foundation might award a Givers Gain Grant.

Suddenly I felt a huge shift!

At Mike Brown's funeral service, something was said that reverberated powerfully within me and made me want to do something even bigger.

It went more or less like this: "Our country has the resources to equip our police forces with military-grade equipment, and yet we cannot equip our public schools." oooof. A gut blow. It made me think that if we do not equip our public schools, we are going to feel a need to equip our police force. We will do one or the other.

Too many great teachers in the inner cities of America who are really able to connect with kids are ham-strung in the classroom due to a lack of funding, lack of available resources and lack of updated, repaired facilities. This is screwed up!

Too many teachers who are failing in their own work cannot be replaced with better teachers due to tenure. This is screwed up!

Too many young kids, who love to learn, who love to excel, who love to grow, are becoming bored, tuned out and being picked off by gangs and a cycle of hopelessness and anger is perpetuated. This is screwed up!

Our BNI® Executive Director in Mid-America, Teresa Morris-Simon, has a daughter whose fiancé spent two years with Teach for America. Tiffany told her mother, "Mom, if you could see the conditions of these schools and the state of affairs there, you would be scared for our country's future."

The B Team

Sir Richard Branson's B Team concept has been germinating in my mind and heart ever since I filmed Ivan with Richard last year as they talked about this subject, and now these events in Ferguson have moved me and Ivan to really want to inspire businesses to value inner city education and schools enough to get involved in being a strong partner in effecting positive change.

Plan A is where companies have been driven by the profit motive alone-our current model that needs to be transformed. Plan B seeks to put people and planet alongside profit, according to our conversations with Richard. The B Team vision of the future is "a world in which the purpose of business is to be a driving force for social, environmental and economic benefit." Further, the mission of the B Team is "to catalyze a better way of doing business for the wellbeing of people and the planet." (Read more about the B Team.)

It is TIME for Richard's B Team concept to manifest itself in America for our schools. B Team! Business has the ability, the means and the smarts to come in and do what our government is not doing well. I want to start a movement: Business VOICES (business values our inner city education & schools).

Business VOICES is not going to be an ad for the BNI® Foundation. You already know that we are providing support to teachers for children and education through the BNI® Foundation. Business

VOICES is an appeal for a groundswell of support that crosses corporate lines, state borders and flows into the communities that need our help so desperately. There are many groups who are supporting inner city schools that need more help. There are many ways we can do better and do more. Let's find out how and where we can start this paradigm shift.

I've never started a movement before. I need your help!

I will begin working with influential voices in this nation to inspire and initiate Business VOICES. I have already talked with Richard about how we can plug in with the B Team. It is my commitment to Ferguson, to South-Central LA, to Harlem and many other inner city schools and teachers who need what I have to give-who need what YOU have to give. This fire burning within me to REALLY make a difference in a tangible way actually keeps me up at night. I lie there awake, visioning and dreaming about how we can stand together and open up a flow of resources like this country has never seen before.

I invite you to join me. I invite you to dream, vision and strategize with me to get this grass-roots effort off the ground.

Let's start something that will have a REAL impact for positive change. The youth of our country need to have a chance to break out of the cycle of poverty and hopelessness. Education gives them that chance. And we have the ability to help them. Please, please come along with me to be a part of the solution.

Chapter I

Mindset

Life is not about getting and having.

It's about giving and being

~ Kevin Kruse

Big in Business-Noble Business People

What are the virtues of business people?

The virtue of business people is in the directions or principles business people hold in expanding their business. Business is the exchange of valuable products or services. Business people can be divided into 4 different groups.

1.Noble Business people

2.Small business people

3.Non-profit business people

4.Dishonest business people

Small business people pursue only their own profits. They exchange their products for money. All they care is to be able to survive. That's the concept for normal business people.

Dishonest business people tend to pursue their purpose by hook or by crook. They commit outrageous acts only for their own benefit. This misbehavior gives society the general idea that it is easier for a camel to go through the eye of a needle than for a rich man to enter the kingdom of heaven. We think the benevolent man cannot be rich and vice versa.

Non-profit business people don't target profits; they devote their energy and money for good purposes and good deeds. They are religious groups or humanitarians.

Noble business people hold two common interests. Only when these two interests are met, can they be called noble business people. The first test is "profit" and the other one is "benefit". Noble business people are interested in making money and gaining profit with good intentions in mind at the same time. They use their wealth meaningfully to support their own business, their families, the society, their countries and even the world. They are fair and try to make a difference by benefitting their communities, societies, countries or the world.

Dishonest business people are extremely evil. Nonprofit business people are extremely virtuous. Small business people are neither evil nor virtuous. Only the noble business people are temperate.

However, we must be persistent in our ethics. It may not be easy to maintain. Most business people start with good intentions. Then later on in their lives they are defeated by material desires and overcome by greed. They forget their original intentions and aspirations.

Dishonest business people skimp on the job and stint on materials in order to raise their profits and lower their costs. They add toxic ingredients to foods for better appearance. This kind of aberration should not be tolerated or justified.

Therefore, the spirit of the noble business person is born. We would like to provide patterns to solve the inadequate concepts held by the society regarding business people and to influence more small business people to be ethical in their thinking and actions.

Your attitude decides your altitude. This book is to give its readers a better understanding of the attitude of great and noble business people whose greed has gone. **When everyone is giving, want will be gone. When people can trust each other, there will be peace.**

The spirit of noble business people is "Givers gain®".

Their spirit is to make the world a better place to live.

Givers create meaning for their benefits and give again after they gain. The benefits (profits) allow them the ability to give more. Such a cycle is the spiritual mechanism of noble business people.

The spirit of noble business is love and compassion for all human beings. We hold the same beliefs and want to benefit the whole world.

We represent different roles in life but we all hold the same beliefs and purpose: to try our best to make the world different-a world where people can trust each other and make it a greater place to live. We do not look exactly the same, but we have the same resonance in our souls. Hence, we call ourselves the noble business people.

The Spirit of Taiwan

Taiwan is the birth place of all the characters in this book. It is also the place where we were raised and educated. We hold strong emotional ties with our motherland. It is an indescribable love.

Taiwan, this small island is the place where all these expressive histories happened. We were the immigrants from TangShan (Mainland China). We were the colonies of Holland and Japan and were the final territory the KMT retreated. All of these factors have created a variety of subplots and cultures and a special passion for Taiwan.

What is the spirit of Taiwan? It is the pursuit of continual transformation and surpassing excellence.

To prosper and die for Taiwan should not be a slogan—it should be an action. Like the many hard-working and devoted Taiwanese we've seen at common places in our daily lives. They use their sweat and energy to bring forth prosperity for Taiwan.

We should not be arrogant because we have a small country. Recognition of this fact should create a stronger and more influential country.

Our existence depends on our dedication and value. We cannot accept those who claim to love Taiwan but use toxic ingredients to harm the health of Taiwanese and damage our reputations and credibility. We could not accept those who claim they are Taiwanese but are proud that they own foreign passports. When we see our gold-medal athletes waving our national flag in international competitions, our cheeks stream with tears. **We are Taiwanese who do not easily abandon an opportunity to sing our national anthem.** For the lyrics of our national anthem represent the most significant era of our formative nation, and contains a record of our beautiful economic take off.

The opportunity of meeting other Taiwanese abroad reassures us of the importance of our country. But only when we step back on our shores do we have a stable and steady emotion.

Although Hsu, Hung has worked overseas, he resolutely returns to Taiwan; and although Hsing-Hui Huang has a Master's Degree from Michigan State University she chose to come back to Taiwan to devote her efforts and work for the future of Taiwan.

Many are looking for the spirit of Taiwan but nobody yet has the right answer. We ask ourselves what we have contributed to this island nation. What is your consensus?

We pursue self-reflection and introspection, we try to make progress. We hope the people who live in this land are proud of their

"Beautiful Formosa." After you have finished reading all the stories of our characters you can decide for yourself what the spirit of Taiwan is.

No matter where we are, no matter how difficult it is, no matter what price we have to pay, we strive forward. It is our goal to make "Hello, I'm from Taiwan" the proudest form of self-introduction.

We don't expect all people over the world to consider Taiwan a great country; but we expect Taiwanese to live courageous and intellectual lives.

We don't expect Taiwan to become the most powerful country in the world but we expect it to be an impressive and influential country and for its inhabitants to live their lives with goodness.

Taiwan is our country.

Marketing

Does marketing mean selling? They are not equal. Selling is only a part of marketing. We need to be experts in both skills. **We are not clear about the process and effort it takes for human beings to transform the business model from plundering to exchanging. When human beings learned about the concept of exchanging, it was the beginning of marketing.**

What is marketing? Actually it can be described as the conveyance of a concept. We will make a fortune if we can successfully convey our concept. Read on! We will see!

Why do diapers become necessities for babies? Because of the concept of "disposable"! In the past, having a baby meant countless cloth diapers and washing. When disposable diapers were introduced, most people considered them luxury goods. Now diapers have become necessary consumable products for babies. That is a great example of concept dissemination. Washing machines, dryers, refrigerators are successfully marketed as "convenient" home appliances. When talking about convenience, then the convenience store in Taiwan is the best endorsement. People who shop at a convenience store do not look for bargains. They shop because the store is close to where they live and there is no time limitation. Convenience stores are open 24 hours a day in Taiwan. We can read and buy snacks or drinks at midnight. We won't see people argue because of the higher price at a convenience store, right?

In Taiwan there is now the common scene of every household barbecuing at Chinese Moon festival. It was never a folk custom 30 years ago. But under the influence of a barbecue sauce TV commercial, it became a unique "must do" ceremony at Chinese Moon Festival in Taiwan. (It is only popular in Taiwan.)

There are so many similar ideas like giving chocolates to a lover on Valentine's Day. Wearing or buying carnations for mothers on Mother's Day.

Another major category for concept dissemination is health food. Organic food has become more and more common and has slowly become more accepted by the majority of families because of the concept of preventive medicine generated by its influence. People would rather spend money on health preservation than spend money on medical treatments.

Death can be discussed during daily conversation, people are not afraid to confront this topic anymore. It used to be taboo ten years ago in Taiwan. The idea of arranging funerals or finding graveyards for ourselves is as normal as purchasing life insurance. We can see topics relevant to this on TV commercials, advertisements on buses and so on. What has been marketed? The concept of "dignity after death" has been promoted.

From birth to life, from alive to dead, different stages of life require different needs. Some of these needs are desired, some are discovered and some are created.

These necessities can be skillfully and cleverly developed into unique selling points and be delivered to the public. Once they are disseminated successfully, that is what we call successful marketing.

What is marketing?

Marketing is "implanting" the concept or our selling points into another's mind to exchange for something valuable into our own accounts. That is marketing.

However, the valuable products shouldn't be measured by money only. Money is an added value. The real value for marketing is joy, happiness, glory, accomplishment and word of mouth reputation.

So what is our product or service?

What's the value of it?

Can we create or deliver the concept to our target audience?

Can our concept arouse their shopping desires?

Word of Mouth

There was a famous Chinese poem people used to describe love.

"What is love that people would die for it?"

And I would like to extend this to "word of mouth".

What is it about word of mouth that people spend so much looking for it?

As the Founder and Chief Visionary Officer for BNI®, the world's largest business networking organization, Dr. Ivan Misner® once mentioned, word of mouth is the most efficient way to generate business. However, the skill has never been taught in school.

The 4P's to Marketing Theory by McCarthy are: product, price, place and promotion. They are the fundamental elements of marketing, but it isn't as effective as generating a business through word of mouth. Therefore, I would like to add four more P's plus one R. **These are people, plan, program and play.** We need to have talented professionals to plan and execute. With all details programmed and strategies planned. We will have a standard operating procedure for everyone in our organization. The plans should be played out as computer programs and they should be duplicated perfectly-then executed like a splendid play. Thus the audience will definitely be amazed and applaud our performance. When all 8P's have brought out our implicit qualities, our product or service will be attractive to our target audiences. Moreover, if we could put "relationship" into consideration, doing business with people with whom we have some level of relationship is ten times easier than doing it with cold marketing. People feel safer and more comfortable in doing business with people they know. They can trust us.

If we perfectly deliver our products or services with 8Ps+1R our customers will be so delighted as to exchange their money with us; and that represents the successful completion of the transaction.

Build relationships and provide them with the best consumer experiences they can possibly have. Satisfied customers will give us great product or service reputation and they will testify for us.

Dr. Ivan Misner® once said on Facebook, **"Testimonials are important" as part of the referral process, especial within referral groups! Never underestimate the power of the third party testimonial.**

With no connections, there will be no chance to experience our services! Without product experience, there won't be great word of mouth. If our customers keep telling their friends and people they know, "I've used this person's products personally and I highly recommend that you use it, too because…" it will make a huge difference in how easy the deal can be closed. Whether good or bad, our reputation is everywhere. It is human nature to share experiences. If we do not provide extraordinary and valuable exchange, we will not receive outstanding testimonials. **Think about how we can provide our customers with a super valuable product or service experience.** It is impossible for them not to share and testify for us if they had such a wonderful feeling.

Great word of mouth leads to popularity of our service. It is not luck. It is the attitude of always being prepared to deliver the best possible service.

Some business people have said that not all businesses are in the service industry. That's not correct.

Actually all business people should consider themselves in the service industry. Otherwise, they will neglect the part that great customer service plays in great word of mouth reputation.

Even if we are in manufacturing, we should not only focus on the aspects of demand and supply. We need to promote our products. The ideal closing moment is our best opportunity to perform customer service. Whether we seize this opportunity or not is the key to the next order. If we provide great service quality, we build positive reputation and then create a wonderful business reciprocation system, vice versa.

Every professional should treat their reputation as precious. No matter what profession we are in - politics, entertainment, education, maintaining a good reputation is not an easy task; especially for successful business people. There's a saying in Chinese "Guard and cherish your reputation as birds treasure their feathers."

Word of mouth is like the course of our life becoming a legend to spread. We could choose to leave an obscure word of mouth, a notorious one or a word of mouth that lasts forever. Word of mouth is not merely for gaining business it is an attitude of being responsible for every action we take in life.

When people talk about us and our product, what kind of word of mouth would we like to hear from them?

The Source of Money is more Powerful than Money itself

We all have certain expectations about life, that we have to be "successful" and be "rich". Our society uses money and fortune to measure success.

However, **the source of money is more powerful than money itself and the usage of money is more important than the money.**

We should be able to answer the question "Why do we want to be rich?"

What are we going to do with our money? **Money is just a tool, a tool that we use to achieve the purposes of our life.** If our purpose of life is happiness and the things we enjoy the most are sitting under a tree and enjoying a cup of coffee or tea with our family at the park. We really don't need to be a billionaire. However, if we love to donate a lot of money and do a lot of charity work to help the society. We definitely need to become a billionaire.

Success is the ability to create fortune. The proper usage of money can create a lot of help.

There are two key points to becoming successful:

1.Our attitude

2.Our methods

If we want to be rich then we can't hold onto negative concepts about money! If we want to be rich, we should like rich people. We don't want to become people we dislike.

If we truly believe that rich people are all evil; or the rich can't find true love and rich men usually have more than one wife, then we push ourselves further and further away from money. These are false concepts about successful and rich business people. Find out what our most mistaken concepts are about money and about wealthy business people, delete them and reprogram our minds. **Then ask ourselves what we will do when we are rich and successful.** We provide 42 stories about noble business people who use their abilities to create a positive influence.

Have the correct attitude, don't be the victim.

Another major factor that will hinder us from becoming successful and rich is to victimize ourselves.

The family of a friend of mine had been very wealthy 200 years ago. However, his great great great grandfather gambled and smoked opium and eventually lost the fortune they had. Starting from his great great grandfather to his father, they spent 200 years as victims and complained and complained about their ancestor! It was quite interesting. Why didn't they spend the time and energy they used for curses to regain their own fortune? Imagine that these men and women gathered together all throughout their lifetimes and sighed and cursed and pitied themselves. Those good old days.... Until my friend finally realized that they were too traumatized to take their own responsibility back. They had imprisoned themselves with their ideas about money. If we assign someone else responsibility for our misery, we will lose our ability. For if they do not change then we have no chance to change.

Be the cause rather than the effect side. If all the 42 noble entrepreneurs were defeated by the obstacles they encountered and lost their enthusiasm and passion for goals, we would never see those encouraging and inspiring stories. **"Success is stumbling from failure to failure with no loss of enthusiasm."**-Winston Churchill

Determination

We need to have a burning desire that urges us to take action and move forward. It is called determination: Knowing from the bottom of our heart that we have no other option. The higher our urgency, the higher our income will be. The decision most people make is a "hope" or a "wish". What we define as **a "wish" is having an excuse for not accomplishing our goal.**

Legend has it that when Julius Caesar invaded Celtic Britain, his generals and armies were hesitant because they were exhausted and outnumbered by their enemies. Caesar set fire to his own ships and burned them to ashes in front of his troops so there would be no chance of retreat. **The Romans had only two choices, to win or to die.** They won the battle in three days and went back to Rome on their enemies' ships. We learn from the story that we need to have an urgent reason to drive us toward our goals. **The stronger our decision (desperation) is, the more powerful our motivation will be.**

If we are not as successful as we desire or as wealthy as we want, then we need to check if we have the correct attitude to make the correct decisions.

People don't care about the how until they know the why!-Dr. Ivan Misner®, the Founder and Chief Visionary Officer for BNI®, the world's largest business networking organization

Knowing the reason why we want to be rich and successful is more important than the methods.

See you at the top!

Gentlemen Love Money and They Get it in a Proper Way

We all need money for our better survival. However, what is the true meaning behind money? Money is printed on paper or plastic but what is the difference between a 100 dollar bill and a piece of paper? Most say the difference is its value and they mean different things. Actually, the difference between the two is trust. We accept the printed paper with different values on it because we believe that we can use this piece of paper to exchange with others for the things we need. **The critical meaning behind the dollar bill is Trust.** That's why many people believe in the US dollar because they trust the U.S.A. more than the currency of some other countries.

For instance, my son, Jeremy considers me a terrible cook. He begs me not to prepare anything for him. Every time I suggest cooking dinner for my family they will reject without hesitation. They think to eat the food I cook is a fatal adventure. Jeremy would always comment that trust is earned as I had "surprised" them so many times.

Yes. **Trust is earned.**

If we gather enough trust with our moral behavior and respectable reputation, money will be attracted to us.

Virtue is the source. Fortune is the outcome.

If we want to gather money we have to gather trust.

Trust is gained by our ways of earning money. How can we keep our moral accomplishments and wisdom accomplishments on the way to success?

There is a story in Chinese history called Mencius Accepts Gold. Mencius was born in 372 B.C. and died in 289 B.C. He was a follower of Confucius in a later generation. He traveled country to country promoting his philosophy of managing the country and becoming a good king for more than twenty years. One time Mencius visited the Kingdom of Chi. The king was known for not being a good son. He had an awful reputation of violating the customary obligations of a child to a parent.

During his stay in Chi the king gave Mencius 100 pounds of gold as a gift. Mencius rejected his offer without hesitation and left the kingdom.

He later traveled to two other different kingdoms. One King Song gave him 70 pounds gold and he accepted it and when he was at the Kingdom of Xue, the king gave him 50 pounds of gold and he also accepted it.

His pupils were confused about why he wouldn't accept the first 100 pounds of gold offered by King Chi but accepted the 70 pounds of gold from King Song and 50 pounds of gold from King Xue. What was the principle behind Mencius's choice and how to judge from right to wrong?

Mencius explained "Actually, to accept or not to accept are both right manners. They match the requirements of etiquette. When I was in the Song Kingdom, I was leaving for my journey and we should always present gifts to those who travel afar. King Song gave me travel expenses; I had no reason to reject him. When I was at Xue Kingdom, the king knew I needed money for weapons to protect ourselves and for the safety of our trip. It was help from a friend, why should I reject him? However it was a completely different case when we were in Chi. King Chi gave me money for no reason. This was bribery. He wanted to use his money to encourage me to say good things about him. My honor can't be bought!

That was the guideline for Mencius in how to acquire money. **We reflect from history to gain wisdom.** The story of Mencius Accepts Gold explains one very important principle.

We should accept money when we deserve it. Don't feel embarrassed to ask or accept. However, if it is money we shouldn't take, it doesn't matter how much, we must reject it at once.

"Gentlemen love money and they get it in a proper way," was the precious advice of our Chinese ancestor. We should gain our wealth through honesty and hard work. We should follow the ethic. Trust is

the correct track to run our life.

Accumulate Trust.

Before we act we must ask ourselves whether it will increase our Trust account or will it cause our Trust account to become bankrupt?

Trust is the benevolent rule for business.

Culture-Code of Honor

The definition of culture is "the generic term of the spirit and the result of material created during the historical development of human society," such as knowledge, belief, value and regulations.

Our thoughts become our character. Our character becomes our behavior. The common behaviors of a group become belief. The common beliefs become the culture.

The culture of a group or an organization should be known and implemented by every member. Let's try to recall the culture of McDonald's, Starbucks or Coca Cola! Do they pop into our minds immediately? How about the culture of our organizations? Do we have one? Is it known by all of us?

The culture of a group indicates the belief and gives the focus of the group. Some groups focus on honesty and integrity. Some groups focus on love. Some groups believe in "Givers gain®." It is like the lighthouse for that group, and its members behave accordingly.

The culture of World-English is "B.I.G." This stands for:

1. Be the cause and be responsible.

2. Integrity and inspiring.

3. Gratitude and benefit.

Every member in our team holds the attitude that they are responsible for everything that happens in their life. It is so much easier and relaxing to manage if we all follow the spirit and culture of our organization.

We also have a code of Honor extending from our culture. It is as follows:

1.Top Quality Attitude

Smile often. Praise others. Work hard and learn earnestly. Do not bring personal moods into our teams.

2.Positive Thought

No criticizing. No Blaming. No complaining. No mentioning any negativity. All negativity stops here.

3.Great Intention

Be determined and believe in our teams.

4.Fine Image

Neat and clean appearance. Speak with certainty. Walk upright with full confidence.

5.Perfection

Love challenges. Coordinate closely. Never give up.

6.Spontaneous

Pay attention to small details. Do not wait for others to remind us.

7.Ownership

Do not ask what the team can do for us, but ask what we can do for the team!

8.Optimal condition

Always be energetic in public. Negative emotion should not last longer than 30 minutes in private.

9.Be On Time.

Respect our time and respect others' time as well. Put the discipline of the team in first place. It's our commitment to each other.

10.Be Happy Every Day.

The quality of our life depends on our happiness. Respect individual differences at the same time.

Guided by Da-Shu Wu, the founder of the Sea Biscuit Club.

These are the cultures and Codes of Honor for our teams. What are yours?

It is never too late to start creating and setting up a culture.

Confront it

During our progress to success, we will always encounter problems and feel pressured. In Chinese, there's a metaphor for "stop", we call it "bottle neck" or "lid for a bottle".

Because of problems, we then stop moving toward our goals or purposes in life. And people in a whole group will stop taking action toward the goals of their group. Vision and goals are the energy for life. We always go through tough problems and learn from them.

Remember, **successful people do not complain or blame. They take action.** However, we lead because we want to help others to solve their problems but can't solve them. After these failures we mistakenly believe it will be safer and easier not to be the one in charge. We don't have to make decisions; we don't have to be responsible for anything.

For example, someone in an organization chooses the wrong restaurant and everyone blames him. He would think to himself, "I won't be the one to decide anymore." They start to blame. They say "They told me to…" and start to regret about their decision.

If "they" don't change or solve the problem, all we can do is be held in position like a "bottle neck" or stopped by the "lid of the bottle" and be a victim of life or an organization.

We should stop complaining.

(**The definition of complain to us is: "If we say something and the problem remains unsolved,"** by my best friend, Da-Shu Wu.)

Look at our failures, our mistakes in our life and in our organizations, ask ourselves for what can we be responsible.

As Meryl Streep says in the movie, Iron Lady, **"If you want to change the party, lead it. If you want to change the country, lead it."**

Use problems in life as the ingredients in the pressure cooker and turn them into the most delicious dish we have ever tasted. The can opener is in our hands. Our lives or the results of our organizations are in our hands.

Don't be measured by the number of our complaints. Be measured by what we accomplish.

Cheers!

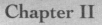

Chapter II

Creating an
Effective Network

System

When anything in this world enters its standard track and proceeds smoothly; then gets into a mechanism and operates naturally, it has formed its own system.

We have heard the word "system", but how much do we understand about the definition of "system". Is it merely a vague and ambiguous concept?

The dictionary definition of system is: "a group of related parts that work together as a whole for a particular purpose; they follow a set of planned rules for operation and complete tasks that require mutuality.

The word "system" originated from Greek syn- 'together' + histanai 'to cause to stand' = 'cause to stand together'.

System should be understood as entirety or alliance. Systems can be divided into two categories "Nature systems" or "Man-made systems".

Nature systems include the human body system, ecosystems,atmospheric systems and water cycle systems. Man-made systems are those systems people create or produce for better living such as electronic systems, social systems, etc. The final product and the processes inside a system should have worldwide standards. For example, McDonald's certainly doesn't sell the healthiest or most delicious food in the world. However, we can be certain about what to expect when we order a box of chicken nuggets. It will meet our expectation no matter what part of the world we are in.

Starbucks is another example. In 2015, I was in a Starbucks café on the island of Aruba in the Caribbean. My friend spilled my coffee and though we didn't speak the language, we went to their counter and showed them the empty cup and the wet floor. We were able to get a refill because we knew the standardized rules at Starbucks. We know what to expect and we know what the results will be if we have a system. **A successful system means the result is guaranteed and the final product will be the same.**

For example if we are a member of Toastmasters, no matter where we are or what language we speak, if we know the time, we can know the procedure or program of the meeting.

That's a system.

In a system, all the members speak the same terms, do the same things. The routines are formulated and repeated over and over.

If we are a member of the world's largest networking organization, BNI® and if we understand their "Givers gain®" culture and follow the fundamental skill set, we will achieve the goal of the organization which is: Members make more money.

That's the most fundamental requirement of a system, a standard program with a guarantee of success.

A system means the result is predictable and under good control. We all need systems to prosper and flourish.

What is the system for our company or organization?

Choose your Environment

In our Chinese Three Character Classic, a 13th century reading primer consisting of Confucian tenets it says, **"When we were born our personalities were of a kind and similar but because of our different growing environments, we formed different personalities. We need to be very cautious in choosing our environments and friends."**

A great poet and politician named Ou-Yang, Xiu once commented that different environments provide different influences: **"Proximity to cinnabar makes you red; Proximity to pitch makes you black."**

If we make friends with noble people we will be nurtured. If we make friends with substandard people we might receive unexpected losses and be implicated with their mistakes.

There is another supporting story for cautiously choosing our environment. When Mencius (372 BC-289 BC), Confucian philosopher second only to Confucius, was growing up, he and his mother lived near a cemetery. Little Mencius watched the funeral processions every day and began to imitate the ceremonies. He buried coffins and built tombs in the sand in the playground. His mother noticed the impact that living by the cemetery was having on her son and so moved to a nearby market place. Soon Mencius picked up the selling sounds of the street vendors and began welcoming people to his home. His mother decided to move again. This time they moved nearby to a school and Mencius learned bowing and etiquette and advanced and retreated graciously. He behaved and became a diligent and hardworking student and learned from the grandsons of Confucius and finally became a famous Confucian master.

We need to carefully select our environments. Watch carefully what influences our minds. As Zhuge Liang, the prime minister and military leader of Shu Han once wrote in his Chu Shi Biao, **"Close to sage and virtuous officials and away from wicked people. That is the reason why the Han Dynasty is so thriving and prosperous."**

The environment and people we choose to be connected with will contribute different causalities.

We as noble entrepreneurs should be aware of the impact of these factors. **If we are close to funeral business people, our focus will be on death. If we are close to educationalists, our focus will be on learning and knowledge. Imagine what will be our attention when we surround ourselves with a group of 50-60 successful and noble entrepreneurs?**

Generating Referrals in Referral Groups

Actually, no other form for referrals is more powerful than word of mouth. **The most powerful team referrals are generated through the cooperation and collaboration of different quality business professionals.** We need to understand the true meaning of referral to be able to discuss it. In recent years, a variety of marketing models and theories have been used and spread. For example: Experiential Marketing, Internet Shopping Malls, App Stores, etc. And among these a structured, positive and professional referral marketing program was founded 30 years ago in America and is now thriving in Taiwan.

Word of mouth marketing is not a mechanism. There is no secret to success in referral marketing. We need to look at the vision and mission of the organization in which we participate. We need to look into ourselves, our partners, our group, our purpose and our systems for generating business.

Take a baseball team as an example. We can be the owner of a baseball team, even though we have never been a baseball player in our life. However, we can't be the coach. And a coach can't be a player or a referee at the same time. **In a team, every player should have** their own expertise and cooperate and support each other to strike for victory. That's why it's a team.

It should be required that there is at least one professional from each industry on the team. **The basic principal for a successful group referral is that every profession should be a symbiosis - cooperation without competition - to build trust amongst members.**

Therefore, we need to have the "right" team members with the correct attitude. A solid and thorough review system is necessary to ensure that every member of the team can assist each other, and to avoid ruining the original foundation. **As the Founder and Chief Visionary Officer for BNI®, the world's largest business networking organization, Dr. Ivan Misner® once said, "A members is not just anyone who is able to fog the mirror."** We should review all applicants with an attitude that our whole group is in a room with a one-way door. Once we let them in we are going to spend the rest of our lives working with them.

And we must be very precise about how are we going to deliver our products or services to make others understand our business and how they can help us in a short period of time. (Like 60 seconds of self-introduction). If we can't introduce ourselves clearly and attractively enough to make a connection with our team members or arouse their "desire" to learn more about our business, how can we expect to have business within our group? **Delivering a perfect self-**

introduction or presentation is very critical in generating referrals.

Doing "one to one" interviewers or visiting our partners increases understanding and connection with each other.

Forming acquaintances to generate referrals takes time and experience to build up enough trust. Referrals occur when true trust has been built, because we are responsible for what and who we recommend-we are risking our own reputation.

After the referral, we need to follow through with perfect service and satisfied customers. As long as our service is great, it will touch the clients' hearts and we will have outstanding word of mouth. Eventually, there will be third party referrals and referrals after referrals. On the other hand, if the service is not satisfying, members need to communicate face to face in detail. Don't complain behind their back.

Take responsibility to solve the unsatisfactory results. If we have members who are not willing to communicate or improve their attitude and remain unchanged, then we should cancel their membership or stop cooperating with them. Sometimes subtraction equals addition. Each member should hold high standards for himself or herself. The prosperity of the whole group is in our own hands.

Taiwanese are people full of hospitality. To be able to do business with Taiwanese, we need to invest our time and be interested in making friends.

Emotion, reason and law are the order for principles we hold in making decisions. We are not completely goal or business oriented. We like to meet people in person, such as having coffee or enjoying meals together. We don't consider this kind of meet-up as a waste of time but a process of building affinity and consensus through communication.

There is a saying that it is more useful to make a phone call than ten emails. It is better to meet in person than ten phone calls and it is more effective to eat together than ten times meeting for coffee.

After increasing the degree of understanding and trust, long-term meaningful relationships start to develop and cooperation becomes much easier. We will find we naturally recommend our members, products or services to families and friends around us. This kind of referral is done sincerely rather than creating a hypocritical or superficial social impression. Such a marketing effect is formed unconsciously. It is selling without selling skills.

That's what we expect from group referrals through word of mouth. The result of one plus one is greater than two. The explosive force of the whole group will be invincible and will triumph in every sale and win every referral.

The easiest way to do business is through word of mouth. And to be able to have enough word of mouth, we need to have trust and meaningful, long-term relationships.

Support

We are easily moved by a good deed a stranger does. However, we often take the good deeds done for us by our family, friends or team members for granted. We forget to show our gratitude. We neglect the fact that there no such thing as a free lunch. No one is obligated to help for we all have the power of self-determination. We should cherish and be grateful when someone lends their hand to us.

Chinese hold a belief in mind that, **"If we receive one drop of water, we should give them a spring in return."** That's the law of reciprocity. The people who gave us life are our parents. The people our parents gave birth to are our brothers or sisters. People who we marry are our spouses. People we give birth to are our children. People who we are related to are our relatives. People who care about us are called friends. People who share the same visions and goals are allies.

However, there is one condition that can bind people together in a continuous and collaborative relationship and that is when their "hearts" are together. There must be a common purpose, a common vision, a common goal and pursuing it for the same result. Under these circumstances we can consider our hearts are bound. This power is called support. Under the circumstances of willingness to understand and help each other, we give our support and we appreciate the support we receive. Out of gratitude we keep on supporting and giving. We must appreciate the opportunity to serve that our partners give us.

The first step to showing our appreciation is to deliver service professionally. Providing the most outstanding and satisfying performance possible and making our partners proud of us. Thus referrals will happen over and over.

The second step to showing our appreciation is to get a deeper understanding of our partners, their goals, accomplishments, interests, networks and skills-knowing how to help them to achieve their goals and realize their dream referrals. Referrals should be what they need, not our own assumptions. However, the occurrence of referrals is like farming, it doesn't necessary generate immediately, it takes meaningful relationships, of watering and fertilizing. When the nutrients are enough, the fruit will ripen and real referrals will happen.

The third step to showing appreciation is to figure out how to benefit each other's business. Like combining each other's advantages and forming a power team to innovate new marketing opportunities and create new markets. This will be the ideal scene for giving and gaining support, taking place simultaneously. By that time, it doesn't matter who gives or who gains first. It is planting, farming and harvesting together.

When members can team up and accomplish with each other and utilize each other's efforts to the peak of glory, that is the highest level of cooperation and we can call them a power team. When the group grows and becomes larger we do not worry about where the referral will come from. They will come automatically.

One-shot type of referrals can be described as social activity. Endless referrals come from endless commitment. If we are not satisfied with the amount of referral business we receive in our group or organization, we should ask ourselves "how or where can I improve myself" instead of blaming others.

Referrals comes from

- The belief and action of "Givers Gain®"
- The deeper understanding and cooperation of "one to one" meetings
- The guests our members invite
- The commitment of the teams
- Credibility through time and trust
- The service qualities we provide
- Our word of mouth reputations
- Our visibility and brand awareness and recall rate
- The law of reciprocity

- The products of our cooperative system

Where does referral come from?

It comes from our VCP® (Visibility, Credibility & Profitability).

It comes from our commitment.

It comes from us.

Kung Fu

The classic wisdom of the Chinese often impresses foreigners. Chinese Kung Fu is the best representation of martial arts.

How to be a Kung Fu master? We need to practice "Qi", and then we must train our minds to stay focused. After many years of hard work learning the fundamentals, we can finally master the techniques and be able to perform truly exquisite combinations of strength and beauty.

Everything we learned has its own basic requirements. To be a chef we need to be a master of knives. To be a great singer we need to master ourselves vocally. To be a great lecturer we need to master speaking. The same rules apply to being a master in generating business.

- Show up early and regularly
- Self-preparation
- Support partners
- Expand our circle of influence

• **Keep learning**

The purpose and measures to practice and apply are described as follows:

A. Show up early and regularly

"Your behavior determines your future in business." Da Shu Wu (Hsing-Hui's coach and friend for life).

Keeping our promise is a basic requirement. Be there on time. Deliver the products on time. Pay our bills on time. Be able to stick to our word and behavior is the first step to credibility and reputation.

"Being on time" is the guardian angel of commitments.

"Being late" is the devil of breaking our commitments.

In an organization, to show up on time and regularly is the most fundamental thing. If we can't even manage ourselves, we are showing no sincerity and sending a message that we are not reliable. It is like the filming of a movie, how do we position our character? Do we consider ourselves a major character or just a minor role? Our absence shows our ignorance and pays no respect to others. Most importantly, we are downgrading ourselves. If that is our attitude, then we will never have an influential role in the organization.

Conversely, even if we begin in a role such as a clown, a supporting role; because of our dedication and respect for our part, we will be more dazzling and impressive than the less earnest players. We might become the next main character. Trust is earned, it can't be bought.

B. Self preparation.

"Always be ready for success."-Dr. Ivan Misner®, the Founder and Chief Visionary Officer for BNI®, the world's largest business networking organization

We need to be prepared. If there is a chance for us to do a self introduction to our ideal clients and we only have one minute, what are we going to say? What will be the first twelve words from our mouth? How are TV commercials so short but so effective? Can we be as effective and impressive?

A lot of people can spend hours and hours talking about themselves; however, they can't introduce themselves in thirty seconds. We need to have a different version to present ourselves according to different time limits. It may be three minutes or 60 seconds or even more challenging, a 25 second version. Make sure we know our unique selling points and the most efficient way to increase people's desire to know us or to use our products or services. Then we need to practice it over and over.

In Taiwan, I grab the chance to practice when I'm waiting at red lights. Usually there is an LED light counting down the number of seconds and I use that as my timer to practice my presentation again and again. There is a saying in Chinese, "It takes ten years of practice to have ten perfect minutes on stage." Because of this practice, I was able to gain a lot of attention at different international conferences. I was always the first one to volunteer when a self-introduction was asked for by the host. It left people with a professional "impression" about me.

C. Support partners

"He who loves others is constantly loved by them"-Mencius, Confucian philosopher second only to Confucius.

"If we help enough people to become successful, we will eventually become successful ourselves"-Dr. Ivan Misner®, the Founder and Chief Visionary Officer for BNI®, the world's largest business networking organization

It is the law of reciprocity. We treat people the way we want to be treated then the good intention will come back to us. We want others to introduce business to us so we should introduce business to others first.

If we have a demand for certain products or services, we should give the business to our partners in our organizations. The one who receives the business should deliver outstanding service. It can be called first layer referrals. We will pass business to the partners who are accountable to friends we know, this is called second layer referrals. Then the wonderful effect will continue to the third layers or the fourth layers, etc. Then the support will come back to us like a boomerang. Sometimes we won't even know where all this business is coming from.

Giving support and providing referrals is not to be rewarded, it is the habit of contributing to our organization and partners. Give will not gain immediately but to gain we definitely have to give in advance. Just like working hard does not guarantee our success, but to succeed we have to work hard.

D. Expand our circle of influence

To invite people to come as visitors to our organization is not selling. It is passionately sharing helpful information and connecting business people together for future cooperation. Therefore, we should not be hindered by the worries of being rejected. It is a pressure-free topic and if we use it properly we not only benefit our organizations, but also improve our own skills in expanding our own business.

Inviting is not equal to agreeing to come. Agreeing to come is not equal to showing up. Showing up is not equal to joining our organization. What matters is that we keep on showing our teammates our personal influence and dissemination ability. Many will complain that the meeting time is not suitable for their guests to come. We either underestimate our influence or our intention to contribute. Reprogram ourselves so that it is very easy to invite guests. Remember, where there is no power to execute there will be no competitive strength. When there is a will there is a way.

E. Keep Learning

There is a saying in Chinese, **"The two greatest tragedies in lives are: to stop loving after we get married and to stop learning after we graduate."** People who think they know everything know nothing because they will always deal with their lives in the same old ways and then get the same old results.

Members of the world's largest networking organization, BNI®, believe in the principle of "learn more and earn more".

The richest person in China, Chi Chen Li says that there are three types of money, the more we spend the more we make. The first spending type is to invest in ourselves for our personal growth. The situation will be the same. In Chi Chen Li's Strategies of Business, Chapter One he talks about no matter how hard he worked, he never quit learning Cantonese and English. He learned Cantonese to base himself in Hong Kong. He learned English to do international exchange. One of the major reasons he became the "king of plastic flowers" was the valuable information he acquired from the English version magazine "Plastic".

If we put Bill Gates in Africa without giving him any money we are pretty sure he will soon become one of the richest men in the world anyway, for he will never lose his wisdom. In other words, investing the money in our wallets, in our minds is the best and most secure investment. Intelligent people know that learning from others' experiences to avoid making mistakes and achieving success is the fastest and safest way. The other type of spending money is spending money on showing gratitude to our parents and spending money on contribution to the society.

To me, learning means to live a better life. **Our speed of learning equals our speed of becoming successful.**

A lot of the confusion in life is caused by ignorance or false information we have accumulated before. Through learning we have a clearer understanding of what caused the confusions and problems in our lives and in our businesses. With correct knowledge we can make better decisions and have more control over our lives. We will achieve order in life and in our businesses, and we will feel less anxious and depressed. By increasing my knowledge I also increase my value and I can exchange more income.

We need to sharpen our axes over and over. The definition of luck to me is the ability to control and predict our future.

I have seen many members at my organization apply the knowledge they learn here and double or triple their income. In order to create better futures, we should always keep on learning. We can never over emphasize the power of knowledge.

Expansion

We can choose to fight alone and be the lone wolves.

However, we need an army troop for battles. How can our armies win over without a strong armed force? Many people are studying the correct ways to do business. Sometimes we use the metaphor of doing business as fighting a battle.

We need extremely strong teams in order to win. That's the most critical part. So recruiting more qualified professionals is one major task we can't ignore. What we mean here is to recruit through inviting guests to participate in our meetings. By doing this, we expand our influence.

What kind of soldiers should we recruit and what kind of horses should we buy? What kind of guests should we invite?

Those who can help build our credibility.

Those who can connect with others.

Those who can help our teams.

These are the qualified quests to invite to our meeting.

When we recruit (invite), we not only focus on those who are close to us, we should also invite those nodding acquaintances and use these opportunities to turn them into friends. Build the relationship from unknown to known, from strangers to partners. Invite guests from our circle of influence and help others to gain business. The favor will come back to us in the near future. We make recruiting into a habit. Make it coherent to our centripetal force for our team. Imaging if we have a team of 10,000, members would we feel "devastating pain" if we lost two of them? What would the feeling be if we only have a team of three and we lose two? We should have a bigger base of teammates.

The benefits of inviting guests to our regular meeting are:

- It will increase our communication skills and our ability in persuasion.
- It is the safest topic to start a conversation.
- It will increase our credibility. One testimonial from others is better than 1,000 sentences promoting ourselves.
- Our contribution will be recognized by our team.
- We should have the mindset that "guests are equal to our clients". Inviting guests is expanding our own business.

The tools we could use:

Use team songs, uniforms, logos, pins, suppliers, invitation cards and greeting cards to attract attention and create topics.

Free tools:

Facebook, WeChat, Line

Propaganda tags with exclusive websites:

Electronic greeting cards for New Years, Valentine's Day, Mother's Day, Father's Day, etc.

Five-minute professional speech invitations

Share stories of success

Where we walk, leave our mark.

If we work hard enough, our hard work

will be paid back.

Hsu, Hung would like to share my "like>> on Facebook as a marketing strategy.

To praise is one of the ways of "Givers gain®".

Don't be so stingy. It costs nothing to praise others.

To praise others online will increase our popularity.

It will increase our visibility and our exposure rate and promote our business.

It is a virtue to praise or press the "like" button on Facebook.

The "like" marketing strategy actually creates a lot of opportunities for recruiting or inviting guests.

Conclusion:

It is easier for larger teams to attract talented and capable professionals to join. That's the influence generated by the atmosphere. The atmosphere formed by the team is exciting, touching and full of energy. We turn the feeling into an impulse and then take action. Then guests become joint partners of the teams and the new partners bring more guests. It enhances positive circulation. Our group will grow stronger and stronger. The success of the enterprise doesn't count on any single individual. The competence of a ball team is not decided by one single star player. A powerful nation is not founded by one hero.

We should always keep the idea of recruiting positive and qualified team players in our mind.

Let's unite together and be invincible.

If we unite together we can be invincible.

Cooperate Without Competitions -Everyone Matters

Three monks ran into each other in a dilapidated temple. They saw that this once flourishing temple now had its tiles broken and its walls crumbling. All they saw was a deserted and desolate scene. They tried to figure out the reason why it had become so run-down.

Monk A said, "It must be because the monks were not sincere enough so their prayers were ineffective."

Monk B said, "It must be that the monks were not hard working enough so there were no properties."

Monk C said, "It must be the monks did not pay respect to Buddha so they didn't have many Buddhist doctrines."

Thus Monk A started to pray and chanted the Buddhist texts with heart and soul. Monk B started to raise funds to repair the temple and gilded the Buddha statues. Monk C lectured on Buddhist texts and cultivated his moral character. Pretty soon the temple started to attract thousands of Buddhist worshipers and it became quite prosperous and returned to its glory and fame.

"It was because I worship Buddha so sincerely that Buddha has blessed us," Monk A considered as his offering. "It was because I manage so well that we have many properties now," Monk B thought it was his contribution. "It was because I urged virtue and promoted it so we have so many Buddhist worshipers," Monk C claimed the credit for himself.

The three monks fought day and night about who was the critical one to give their outstanding performance and the grandeur of the temple gradually began to fade. One day the three of them decided to go their separate ways. They finally came to a consistent conclusion. The abandonment of the temple was not because of the insincere monks nor the lazy monks nor the disrespectful monks. **It was because the non-cooperation of all the monks.**

The moral behind this story is: **If every member of our society or organization performs to the best of our abilities and we present our specialties, the prosperity of the society or organization is guaranteed.** In contrast, if all we see are the disadvantages of others, if we blame and find fault, then no matter how talented we are, we will never achieve the success we desire. **Every single one of us matters.**

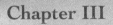

Chapter III

Building Productive
Relationship

Accountability

We all want to do business with people who are accountable. For we want to spend our time and money with people who are reliable and predictable. No one wants to risk their lives and money.

There are five stable points we could apply in judging accountability.

1.No doubt.

In buying and selling, we desire to deal with people we can count on. We know they can control their behavior in a good way. When they say they will show up at 6:30am, they do so. When they promise to deliver the products on May 1ˢᵗ they keep their promise and deliver them.

Nowadays, people tend to skip stages in selling. They neglect the fact that we want to do business with people we can trust. It takes time to build reliable and predictable relationships. Sometimes we meet people only for the first time and we can hardly remember their names yet they are ready to sell. This kind of forceful selling method sometimes frightens us and pushes us away from purchasing. We don't have any social credit (accountability) with each other, not to mention purchasing behavior.

It's not a problem of the product itself. It's not a question of any necessity. It's the ways the products or services are delivered. Picture the apple being sold by the old lady in *Snow White*. Would you buy or eat it?

Therefore, we need to act reasonably in our organizations, companies or groups. Our members are our best business partners (referral sources). Leave them with the impression that they can count on us.

2.No worries.

We are concerned about what's going to happen next. We would love to build long-term, meaningful relationships with people who have wonderful records of honesty and integrity. **After all, their behavior is predictable and we won't get hurt or betrayed when providing them with business.** There's a story in "Romance of the Three Kingdoms" (Three Kingdoms Period 200-280) Lu Bu was a brave and fierce general and warlord who vowed loyalty and devotion to Dong Zhuo, the top general of the late Han period. Lu Bu gave Dong Zhuo succor in usurping power and murdering the empress dowager and the child emperor of Han. However, Lu Bu killed Dong Zhuo later over a woman name Diao Chan, one of the Four Legendary Beauties. The Han dynasty then broke into three kingdoms and Lu Bu was defeated by Cao Cao, the founder and first king of Cao Wei and became his prisoner. Cao Cao was hesitant about whether to execute

Lu Bu for he was a rare and excellent general. He asked his advisors for suggestions and they said "Look what he did to his lord, Dong Zhuo. Can you trust him?" Lu Bu was executed because of his unreliability and disloyalty. **It doesn't matter how talented one is. If he does not have accountability, this person won't generate great business.**

3.Follow through.

People with accountability do not procrastinate. We think of an idea, we take action and we complete it thoroughly. If there's a business opportunity, we not only follow up, we follow through. Whatever it takes and however long it lasts, we make sure things get done. No excuses.

4.Go into action.

We love what we do. Also we have a lot of certainty about our own ability and we are sure that we are competent leaders. Therefore, we don't waste time in making decisions. We make a decision then we execute it. We take the proper actions to accomplish our decisions at high speed.

5.Insist on perfection.

We continue to make things go the way they should and we carry on even when they don't. We handle situations and conditions.

We figure out what to do and continue to create the best results. We hold the belief that "perfect is perfect" and don't stop until we reach perfection. We know we can't be losers as long as we don't give up.

We don't grow money. Money is given to us. We need to build our accountability in order to start getting business from others. Without accountability, it's impossible for sane people to want to buy from us.

Leadership

It takes hard work and skill to establish a company or an organization. Most companies go out of business within the first three years. Therefore, there are certain things leaders need to learn and know to establish a successful organization.

To be successful leaders we need to have a clearly defined organization pattern. We need to know where to assign the right people to the right positions, what our most competitive and desirable products are, how to produce and disseminate the products and create satisfied customers and how to generate business to support the whole organization. We do not necessarily need to perform any of the individual positions in our organization, but we need to be able to oversee, to identify the different departments and divisions and, as needed to correct and improve. We determine the vision and mission of the organization and put them all in order. We manage the organization and we execute our mission.

A qualified leader should have at least the following attributes:

1. Adoration

Our subordinates will follow us contently. Our executives promote us because they like and trust us. If our subordinates do not like us, no matter how true our words, they won't be carried out.

2. Cognition

We should have the ability to thoroughly understand the current condition of the organization and to make correct decisions and implement suitable strategies.

3. Accept and give communication

When our co-workers come to us with their problems we should be able to acknowledge them without giving them the solutions or handling the problems for them. Instead we should have the wisdom to ask them the correct questions and lead them to have the ability to solve their problems by themselves. Self-determination is an important quality for competent workers.

4. Be gracious; and never take assistance for granted

This should be the culture of our whole organization and as a leader we should set the right example. Our teammates need recognition and acknowledgement. Reward the high performers and these activities will motivate others in a positive way. Great leaders are confident and not afraid to halo their teammates.

There is an inspiring Chinese story by "Zhuangzi" (369-286 BC), a Daoist author. It uses the metaphor of "principles for a robber" to point out the five qualifications of a great leader.

In ancient times, there was a famous robber named Zhi. His disciples once asked him, "Are there rules and regulations to being a robber?" Zhi replied, "Is there any place in this world where you can go without rules and regulations?

If one wants to be the best robber, he must be an intelligent person to be able to predict what kind of treasure there is and where it is hidden.

He must be a smart person to be able to decide when to take action.

He must be a courageous person to be the first one to break in.

He must be a reliable person to be the last one to retreat from the site.

And he must be an equitable person to distribute the stolen property fairly. There is none who cannot ignore these five rules and be the best robber in the world. "

We can always find wisdom from our Chinese ancestors.

For Zhuangzi, the five required elements to being a great leader are knowledge, intelligence, courage, brotherhood, and justice. Even robbers have to follow these principles, not to mention leaders of companies and organizations.

The best leaders set an example and inspire others to follow.

Can we consider ourselves as leaders who meet all these requirements?

Lead Ourselves

"Self, family, country and then the world" is a well known precept for leaders in Chinese culture. It provides increasing zones of responsibility.

Many people want to lead others. However, whether we are with family, at school, in businesses, or in government the first person we must lead is ourselves.

We need to be able to lead our own minds and our behavior, and then we can begin to acquire the ability to be true leaders.

Are we leaders who inspire and walk the talk? **People follow us because of our inspiration, because they are touched by our vision and they admire us or trust us. We are their role models.** Are we leaders likes George Washington, Dr. Martin Luther King or Dr. Sun Yat-sen, the father of the Republic of China?

Will people die for us because of our inspiring dreams?

Are we a leader who orders or threatens? Do our subordinates follow out of fear of punishment? They obey and act because we are more powerful than they. Do they follow because they have no other choice?

Are we leaders like Nero of Rome or Qin Shi Hung, the first emperor of the Qin Dynasty 259-210 BC, known for their tyranny?

True leaders enjoy popular support and the will of the people. They endeavor to lead by their good example. The more influential the leader, the more cautious they are in their thinking and behavior.

In another inspiring story shared by Andrew Hall, the National Director of BNI® China, Hong Kong, Macau and Taiwan. During World War II, both Hitler and Churchill were powerful leaders and orators. They both made very famous speeches. The first aroused Germany to go to war with the rest of Europe; and the second united the whole of England to prevent the invasion by Germany. They were both leaders however, the difference was that Hitler considered himself a hero; and he told his audience that he would lead them to conquer Europe. Hitler emphasized his own power. **On the other hand, Churchill considered himself an inspirer, he used "you" and "we" in his speeches. He encouraged people, and entrusted the mission of protecting England to every British citizen.**

True leaders inspire action rather than demand it; and they don't consider themselves heroes.

As Meryl Streep said as The Right Honorable Margaret Thatcher in the movie The Iron Lady,

Watch your thoughts, for they become words.

Watch your words, for they become actions.

Watch your actions, for they become habits.

Watch your habits, for they become character.

Watch your character, for it becomes your destiny."

Our team members will not trust what they hear from us. They judge our actions and then decide.

Let's be true leaders.

Ownership

Some people say that leadership is like eagles looking down proudly.

Some people say that leadership is like a train—moving forward with speed.

Others say leadership is like water droplets—spreading slowly.

Leadership is a concept, a behavior, a phenomenon and it is often a process.

Leadership is responsibility. In the movie The Iron Lady, The Right Honorable Margaret Thatcher was not satisfied with the situation in her country. Her friend Airey Neave made a suggestion to her, **"If you want to change the party, lead it! If you want to change the country, lead it!!"**

We must stop complaining and acting so cold and detached toward our organizations, our parties and our societies. We must take the baton and lead. We don't have to be somebody to be able to do something - remember the Butterfly Effect theory.

Similar, there was a story shared by Andrew Hall, the National

Director of BNI® China, Hong Kong, Macao and Taiwan.

When Andrew was young, he and his brother had the duty of washing their family car. They complained about this labor especially on chilling cold winter days. Every time they had to wash their family car they could not stop voices broadcasting in their minds. The same thing played over and over until one day when Andrew got to the age when he was able to drive. His grumbling stopped when his father handed him the keys to the family car. It was his car then and Andrew's attitude toward the car completely shifted. From then he washed the car so carefully and attentively no matter how bad the weather conditions were. What made the difference was his state of mind. It was his car. It was no longer the family car.

Ownership is the key. If every worker or member in the organization could have the state of mind that they were the owner of the company, the owner of the organization or the owner of the team, we would assume the responsibility and be happy, because it is ours.

We can be the first water droplet to drop into the lake and the ripples will begin. Start to influence others. If the members in our teams - from the president, finance planner, visitors and host exhibit their ownership and take up the responsibility for the success of our organization, only good things would happen. What kind of difference can we make?

Be the first water droplet that starts to influence and exhibit

leadership by playing our roles well.

Members are not "just members." We should be the best leaders we can be in our positions and shine. Every position is critical and by demonstrating our leadership as much as we can, the more ownership we take, the more influence we create. When everyone agrees to perform at their best, to be the best host or hostess they can, we will eventually achieve a first-class leading position.

We will become the ocean that contains everything!!

Let's be the owner of our own destiny!

The "Right" People

In episode 393 of BNI® podcast "The 7 Things I Learned from Starting a Business".As the Founder and Chief Visionary Officer for BNI®, the world's largest business networking organization, Dr. Ivan Misner® once said "Ignorance on fire is better than knowledge on ice." There is no such thing as the right professional at the right place. It's about the right people. In the early stage of expansion of BNI® National, instead of doing marketing strategy they did networking. They followed people. BNI®was able to expand because members moved to other areas. It's people's intention and attitude rather than anything else.

How to judge the right people from the wrong people? Sometimes, it might be looking at things from a different perspective. We need to have very clearly defined administrative charts and organizing boards to know who to recruit and where to position them.

In a Chinese story, there was a famous and talented son of a noble named Meng Changjun in the Warring States period (475-221 BC). He had more than three thousand followers performing different specialties for him.

During one of his visits to another country, Meng was arrested. He relied on two of his followers who were despised and scorned by all the other followers to escape. One of them stole a white fur coat to bribe the wife of the king to provide them the opportunity to escape and the other one imitated the sound of a rooster to distract the door keeper of the castle. And the door keeper opened the gate earlier than he was supposed to. A thief and a mimicker were the "right" people for that situation and Meng Changjun safely returned to his home country.

Never underestimate the value of any person. Knowledge is power and friends are resources. We never know who they know. Also, what is the standard for choosing the right person?

There is another story in the Records of the Grand Historian by Sima Qian (known as the father of Chinese historiography - 145-86BC). When the king of the Wei Dynasty asked his chancellor about who to choose to be the prime minister between two people who seemed equally qualified, his chancellor replied he would observe these two people's daily behaviors from the following perspectives:

- The people he is usually close to.
- The friends he has when he is rich.
- The people he promotes when he has power.
- The things he didn't do when he was poor.
- The things he preserves during destitute times.

As leaders we could use these standards to see another's basic essence and judge who is more suitable for the position!

From the story above, it tells us to observe his attitude and behavior when he is rich, powerful and humble and we could therefore judge whether he has the right ethic to hold an important post.

We shouldn't do management *in* the organization. We should do management *on* the organization and understand who the right person is to use and spend our time with.

Lead with Virtue and Treat Others With Sincerity

True leaders do not manage in their organizations, they lead by examples. They do not treat their team members as "assets," they do not set rules and regulations to punish or limit them, they treat their team members as their most valuable clients.

Rules and regulation are set to help team members to achieve their goals for business and their purposes in life. The starting points are different.

We need to make sure that we do not do business with "personal emotion". What it takes to do business is "commitment" and "engagement." One thing on which we should be clear is that it is impossible to please everyone in our teams, as the leader of our teams. We should be impartial and fair and guard our integrity. We persist in doing the right things in order to make the right people in our teams like us better.

There is a story from Romance of the Three Kingdoms about a prime minister named Cao Cao who cut his own hair to demonstrate that even a great leader must follow his own orders.

One time, Cao Cao was leading his troops in fighting his enemies during the fall. It was harvest season for wheat and the farmers had hidden away for fear that the troops of Cao Cao would kill them. None of them dared to stay and reap their wheat. After Cao Cao learned this, he issued an imperial edict that he would behead any soldier who dared to trample the wheat fields or hurt any of the farmers; and he made the order known.

As a consequence, the soldiers were cautious when passing the fields not to damage any of the crops. They would even dismount from their horses to pass the fields carefully. The common people of his country profusely praised Cao Cao and his edict. A couple of days later however, Cao Cao was passing a field of wheat when a flying bird frightened his horse. The horse stepped into a field and ruined a swath of wheat. Cao Cao asked to be beheaded but no official dared to enforce his order. Cao Cao replied, "If I cannot follow my own order then who will follow our edicts willingly. How can I lead my army if I am a man who cannot keep his own word." He took out his sword to kill himself but was stopped by his generals.

Later Cao Cao make a pronouncement to his upper, middle and lower armies, "The prime minister trampled the wheat field and should be beheaded. However, he has instead cut his hair as a representation, for he shoulders the responsibility of protecting our country and expanding its territory."

The story of "Cao Cao cuts his hair" has become a metaphor for great leaders who walk the talk.

The moral of this story is that true leaders should lead with virtue and treat others with sincerity.

Addition by Subtraction

We live in a world with people. Lonely people are not happy or successful. We need to learn to cooperate with others in order to become successful.

However, we need to choose who to spend time with and surround ourselves with the right people. Dr. Ivan Misner®, the Founder and Chief Visionary Officer for BNI®, the world's largest business networking organization, once introduced the metaphor that we should choose the people in our network with the attitude that there's only a one-way door for the people who enter our life. They will stay there with us for the rest of our life. There's no way we can avoid them. Imagine having to mingle with someone we dislike or someone who steals our energy whenever we talk to them or see them.

Select our environment and select our partners for life or for a job. There are certain guidelines to wisely choosing our friends.

In Chinese, we have Chinese Astrology, Eight Characters, Physiognomy or Palmistry. However, it is strange to ask people about his/her birthday and time of birth. The easiest and most reliable way is to observe their emotional state.

Our lives are always led and influenced by our emotions. The emotional state of a person is the index of their energy of life. We can predict how much vitality this person has and his/her attitude toward his job, his family, his friends and every aspect of their life.

We hold three different types of emotional state:

1.First Impressions

It's not real. We put masks on ourselves. The best example is the emotional state we use when we are interviewed for a job. Another example is when we are at the early stages of dating and we try our best to show the most desirable parts of us. We need to be skillful to see through this disguised social-emotional state.

What a man should fear is to accept a wrong trade, and what a woman should fear is to marry the wrong man.

2.Temporary emotional state

We feel excited when we hear good news like winning the first prize of the lottery. We feel upset when we see the scratches on our brand new car.

These are temporary emotional states.

3.Real emotional state

Every person tends to hold a permanent or habitual emotional state. We should observe the emotional state of a person and choose our friends or partners cautiously. We can't have positive lives with negative people around. There are some tips we could use to identify the state of a person. We could read his messages or articles he posts on Facebook or blogs. Remember we need to be very objective and not make careless assumptions.

The state of our emotions provides a clue to the communication factor. It would be very difficult to communicate with people who hold fixed emotional states such as lifelessness, hate, fear or anger. These people tend to do or say the wrong things at the wrong time. They will make trouble and not control things well. In other words these people are not reliable and it will be difficult to build meaningful long-term relationships. Their mind and behavior are as changeable as the weather.

We want to spend our time and energy with people, we can trust and do business with. We should be very selective about our members and teammates. **People with high emotional states are interested in things, cheerful and enthusiastic, they are full of vitality and motivation. They are passionate. These are the people with accountability. They walk the talk.**

We should avoid the people who have these traits:

- Don't cooperate with people with heavy personal greed because they can't see the devotion others give. They only care about their own success and results.
- Don't cooperate with people without a mission or a vision as they cut corners for their own benefit. The only purpose for them is to earn money.
- Don't work with people without friendliness. You won't be happy. Fun is the fundamental for everything.
- Stay away from negative people. They will consume your positive energy.
- Don't work with people without principles. The only principle they have is to benefit themselves.
- Don't work with people without gratitude or who forget favors. They will definitely violate justice.

Don't stay in contact with the following people:

- People who do not show filial piety to their parents.
- People who show no respect to others.
- People who are sharp and unkind.
- People who haggle over every ounce and bicker at length over a trivial matters.

- People who are flattering and fawning.

- People who hold no principles when facing authority and cling to the powerful and rich.

- People who hold no empathy.

Cherish these people. Build long term and meaningful relationships with them:

- When cooperating, they will give more benefit to others. Not because they are stupid. It's because they are willing to share.

- People who step out of their way to help. They do extra. Not because they are silly. It's because they know the meaning of responsibility and ownership.

- People who take the initiative to help you. It's not because they owe you. But they treat you as true friends. Many people neglect these simple rules and sometimes people take others' help for granted.

- As Mencius once said we should "Not be shaken by poverty. Not submit to force. And not be corrupted by wealth and honors." These are the standards for betterment and our principles in choosing friends.

- As Confucius said we should choose to partner with people who

are outspoken, forgiving and knowledgeable.

Look for people who have these traits before we invite them into our lives or our organizations. Establish a mental "gate-keeper" to ensure that only the people with high emotional states get through.

I have a friend who worked very hard trying to set up an organization through recruiting owners of different enterprises. He was devoted to the building of his business wholeheartedly for more than six months and was only able to recruit six members. On the night he was ready to quit and give up his business we had a talk and I only made one suggestion, "Look into your friends and indicate who could be the dream stealer and handle that source or cut off that relationship." He did and accordingly his organization grew from six members to twenty-nine members in two months! He said it was luck.

Actually it's the principle of "addition by subtraction".

In order to have a great harvest for fruit farmers, they have to prune the branches that do not bear fruit.

Having the ability to accurately predict the behavior of a business partner, employees or friend before committing to a relationship can lower or avoid the risk of treating people with sincerity in exchange for betrayal.

More doesn't necessarily mean better. Sometimes subtracting the negative dream stealers adds up to productivity and efficiency.

We need to be aware of certain signs. Are we getting sick more often than others? Are we suddenly accident prone? We live our lives on an emotional seesaw. Do we do well one day and badly the next? These signs actually have nothing to do with the gods, fate or the position of the stars. In fact the actual reason behind these phenomena is that we surround ourselves with negative people, people who suck our energy.

Observe the behavior of friends and people we know carefully. We should have the knowledge and skill of knowing how to recognize people who wish us ill; those who should not be our friends.

Trust-I think I can

There is a story I loved to read to my sons, Jonathan and Jeremy when they were little The Little Engine That Could. This story is used to teach children the value of optimism, persistence and hard work. It is also about belief in our own ability and being able to motivate and encourage ourselves when we need to. In the story, a long train must be pulled over a high mountain. All the larger engines refuse the task giving different excuses. In the end the mission is given to the little blue engine. It is willing to try and succeeds in pulling the long train over the mountain while repeating its mantra, "I think I can! I think I can!" The engine's belief in itself drives it to overcome a seemingly impossible task.

When we talk about trust, the Chinese definition is **"Belief without doubt"** and **"Reliable and accountable"**.

To be successful in businesses or in any field, we need to have the ability to believe in ourselves. There is a story about belief without doubt in The Analects of Confucius.

One day, a lord named Fan Tzu-hua was playing on a high platform with his followers. One of them said "Whoever jumps off from here will get one hundred pounds of gold." Every fellow pretended to jump except Shang Qiu-Kai who truly believed it and jumped off from the high platform. He flew in the air as light as a swallow and landed on the ground without any damage. Every spectator felt strange, they pointed to the deep lake and claimed that there was jewelry in the lake and whosoever dove in and found it could own it.

Shang Qiu-Kai believed it again and found the treasure. Everyone screamed and felt amazed. They all thought he had magic power. A few days later, a fire broke out at Fan Tzu-hua's mansion. Fan Tzu-hua told his followers "Whoever can go into the fire can own whatever treasure he rescues from it." Shang Qiu-Kai ran into the fire many times without getting burned. Everyone now believed firmly that he possessed magical powers. One day, one curious fellow finally asked him "What kind of magic power do you have?" Shang Qiu-Kai replied "I don't have any. **The only specialty I have is I never doubted anything. I believe in you.** Whatever you told me to do I did it without hesitation because I considered it real and I didn't consider the damage that could happen to my body. I just believed and focused on completing the task at hand." Then he continued, "However, later I found out you were lying to me all the time. I started to feel suspicious and became cautious. Now I cannot get close to water or fire anymore. The anxiety and fear stops me."

After Confucius learned the story, he commented, **"People who truly believe can move the whole universe. They can move heaven** and earth and achieve anything. Shang Qiu-Kai truly believed without doubt and achieved without hindrance. We have to keep this power in mind."

That is one great example of trust in oneself. The first rule of thumb for magic is to do things without doubt and trust in yourself.

If we can stay focused on accomplishing our goal without doubt we can definitely create an ongoing stream of income.

Yes, I do!
(Earn our Trust!)

What does it take for one person to give their business to us or refer us business? What are we risking when we refer another's business to people who trust us? Who will be damaged the most when we do not perform our best and fail to deliver the best service? **Referring friends or acquaintances to people we do not trust is likely to endanger our own reputation. In the business world, reputation is more important than money.**

It takes many stages to build enough trust in order to generate word of mouth referrals.

Let's take marriage as a metaphor for receiving business. The process is similar. It takes more than trust.

What does it take for one mature man and woman to say "yes" to each other and get married?

Even if there is love at first sight, most marriages go through certain stages of relationship.

Existence

Generally people try to get to know who we are and what we do. They start to notice each other and there might be some interest. We need to do something to get each other's attention and start to date regularly. There is no way for a woman or a man to begin a relationship if we only call her once in a blue moon and say we "love" her/him. We need to cultivate the relationship like a farmer not a hunter.

Performance

The relationship will then move into a stage of reliability. It is more than trust. The definition of trust includes "without doubt" and the definition of reliability includes "we believe firmly". At this stage of our relationship we not only know what each other does and who they are, we are pretty sure we can count on each other. Trust is the foundation and we need to have a certain accountability.

Feedback

Through the fermentation of time, we now both know who we are, what we do and whether we are good at it. The most important fact of all is to now be willing to risk our future happiness and settle down.

The process of obtaining business is similar; we need to build a long-term, meaningful and positive relationship. The most unwelcome behavior is to jump over stages. Imaging that we just meet a lovely girl for the first time and we propose to her immediately. She must be insane to say "yes" to us, right? Or she will think that we are insane and reject us. Everyone has the desire to find their Mr. or Mrs. Right, but we don't feel safe to commit without enough understanding to meet our conditions. The same thing happens in the business world. People want to buy, but nobody wants to be sold. We don't usually buy with an impulsive feeling.

Build and cultivate our relationships and we will eventually get what we want; and remember it is not just what we want. We should have existence, performance and feedback in order to get the "I do".

Exchange and Help

There are social ranks—scholars, farmers, laborers and merchants in Chinese culture.

Why are merchants put at the lowest rank? Why in general do people devalue merchants?

There used to be some misconception about merchants-Merchants are evil and dishonest. They do whatever it takes for their own profit. They are selfish. They cut corners. Laborers and farmers use their hard work to exchange for a living.

Therefore, the major discovery we have here is exchange and help. The public looks down on merchants because they consider there to be an unfair exchange. Merchants make their money "too easily". Merchants are also devalued because of the way they use their money. They don't use their profits to give back to society, or help their society and country to become a better place. It doesn't matter what kind of profession we are. What matters is the method we apply in exchanging our wealth.

Noble entrepreneurs produce and deliver valuable products. They know people will feel cheated if we give them a flawed product or incomplete service.

A product must be able to retain its value and help others achieve better survival. Noble entrepreneurs have the central idea of how to help and how to give more help rather than focusing on only money and profit.

We do not cut our prices or our services; this kind of strategy depreciates our ability. Instead we choose our clients carefully and evaluate whether we can help our clients and provide them what they need. **Our success comes from satisfied customers with an abundant value of exchange.** That is the best strategy to use in generating outstanding word of mouth referrals.

We should establish value rather than compete in price.

Sometimes we are too impatient about the results. We want to get rich quick. Actually, if we keep on doing the correct things and accumulate energy over a certain period of time, the results may amaze us. The route to real success and generating countless referrals is the farming process of farmers. The farmer sows seeds, waters them and applies fertilizer and nothing seems to happen at first. However, the farmers do not give up. They do not dig the soil looking for signs of crops or try to pull up the short sprouts. The farmers are patient, they believe they will reap what they have sown, they know for sure that industriousness and diligent effort will bring them a bumper harvest. That is the way of the law of nature. It takes time but it will come back to us. Let's all be famers who plant help into each other's hearts and exchange our products with good service and our harvest will be guaranteed.

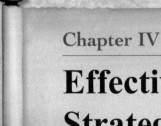

Chapter IV

Effective Marketing Strategies

Lifelong Learning

What is learning? Why should we learn? Most of us pay lip service to learning, for we have accumulated many scary experiences at school. We all agree that learning is important but we hesitate when we need to put it into practice.

Learning is gaining the ability to survive better. Have you ever heard about the story of the lumberjack? It goes like this:

Long, long ago there was a champion lumberjack called John. For almost ten years, he would always cut down more trees than anyone else on the team. When others cut down fifteen trees a day, John would cut down thirty. His speed and skill were miraculous and the other lumberjacks viewed him as their idol-he was so much better than anyone else. The situation continued in this way for years until one day a very tiny but bonny man named Jerry, walked up over the hill and asked to become a part of their team. He was rejected by the other lumberjacks because he was not tall enough or strong enough. But Jerry would not give up. Instead he challenged them, "If I could out-chop your best man, will you hire me?" Everyone thought this was a good laugh, but they agreed. On the day of the challenge, no-one thought highly of Jerry or believed he could win. At the end of the day, John came back with his highest score of thirty-three trees in one day. However, none of the lumberjacks could believe their eyes when they saw that Jerry had cut down thirty-six trees. Jerry was hired immediately and ever since that day he remained the champion of the team. No matter how hard John tried, he could never beat Jerry's record.

John even went to work earlier and stayed longer. But he still could not do it. It seemed impossible to everyone that Jerry could win so easy and that he must be cheating in some way. There was no way he could be beaten and yet Jerry seemed so relaxed in his chopping work.

The lumberjacks devised a scheme to follow Jerry and observe him secretly to discover his secret of success.

They set a team to follow him to watch him work and even followed him home at night. They found out there was no other worker secretly cutting down trees for him; and they even found had had enough energy to play his guitar after dinner. The men were baffled but just when they were about to leave his home, they noticed that Jerry took out his axe and carefully began sharpening it. He sharpened and sharpened his axe until it was able to cut a single hair by dropping it on the edge of the axe. They had discovered his secret! Jerry's speed and skill lay in his axe! Jerry knew that wielding a razor sharp axe was far more important than mere strength.

Abraham Lincoln once said, "If you give me six hours to chop

down trees, I will spend four hours to sharpen my axe". Most of us consume our six hours chopping and neglect the sharpening part.

Through learning we save our time through not making mistakes. We learn from others' experiences. We do not have our whole lives to experience all the mistakes one could possibly make. It is far more effective to learn the right way to do something and to change the false concepts we hold.

To be champions, we need to constantly update our knowledge.

The Founder and Chief Visionary Officer for BNI®, the world's largest business networking organization, Dr. Ivan Misner® emphasizes the importance of training and education. He says, "People don't care about the how until they know the why." That explains why we need to do training and education.

I used to consider training unnecessary and a waste of time but after I joined one of the chapters of the largest networking organization in the world, I was in the leadership team and took part as an education coordinator.

I studied all the available materials and realized that there was a standard operating pattern for the success of any organization or company. Neither the leaders nor their partners can just assume they already know the requirements for success.

We need to be able to communicate thoroughly and make sure

every member in our team can understand the organization's pattern to produce the best results. Knowledge is like water in a basket, it will leak through in time. That's why we need to have regular training sessions arranged to ensure all the fundamental principles are followed precisely.

Regulations are not set to confine or punish members. They are set out to help every member to benefit and get the most out of an organization or a company. It's the accumulated wisdom gained through trial and error.

Training is to explain to the members about the why, like the mission and vision of an organization or a company, and the how, like the correct systems used to the advantage of the organization.

Training can be defined as coaching, giving practical instruction and dispelling doubts and confusions.

As a trainer we need to be able to (a) show them (b) do it with them (c) observe them while practicing (d) direct them and ensure that they can duplicate completely. Therefore practical manuals compiled with standards should be established. The manuals should explain the vision, mission, responsibility, tools and resources step by step in detail. The basic purpose for success should be clear and in written form, organized and made into rules to follow.

If we could apply above formula, then obstacles will become easy to conquer. It is the job of the education training department to guard the future success of the organization.

Create Value

We wonder how to generate business.

Where does business come from?

The story of a dog and a wolf can best describe it.

A dog and a wolf are chatting to each other. The wolf is upset and complains, "I don't understand it. We have so many similarities. We both have fur, a tail and sharp teeth. However, when people talk about you, they are happy and they love you. But when they talk about me they are afraid and think I'm evil."

The wolf was angry and continued his complaint, "Frankly speaking, I am a lot more graceful than you. I can attack and yelp better and you look so dirty and humble with your menial tasks. Why don't people admire me?"

The dog calmly replied, "Mr. Wolf, you have your point. **But people adore me because I provide service to them; I watch the door and play with them. Can you tell me what you have done for people?"**

Mr. Wolf was discomfited and replied, "Why should I work for them? They should praise me and admire me."

The dog shook his head and said, **"You should treat people the way you want to be treated first."**

Many people complain about having unrecognized talents and cannot figure out why no one admires their superior talents or ability. Why are we neglected and isolated? In fact, our value is like that of the dog and the wolf in the story. **It doesn't matter what we have or who we are, what matters is the help we give to others.**

It is not the superior talent and ability we have, it's what we contribute to others with our superiority, talent and ability. If our existence cannot produce happiness in others, then no matter how superior and outstanding we are, it will be in vain.

Let our giving become another's blessing. Let others' gain become our happiness. Let's make the world a better place because of us. Give a little help, lend a hand, listen to others' needs and provide for them.

We will bring about happiness and many wonderful experiences for others.

If we want people to help us, lend a hand first.

If we want business, provide business opportunities first.

If we want to be happy, spread happiness first.

Plans and Programs

As the Founder and Chief Visionary Officer for BNI®, the world's largest business networking organization, Dr. Ivan Misner® said **"A goal without plans is just wishful thinking."** To realize our goal is not simply to make a decision then wait for it to happen. We need to take certain actions to make our goal happen. The accomplishment of a goal involves many subjects and each subject needs to operate in coordination. When the levels cannot coordinate with each other the whole plan will either fail or encounter a lot of obstacles. In any activity, the technique to coordinate all the items and implement them is call management.

When there is one or more than one item failing to support each other and there is disagreement, consensus breaks down and members of the organization will feel frustrated and the energy of the whole organization will be slow, ineffective, unhappy and dull.

When all the items are in symbiosis, there will be great consensus, communication and support. All the usual practices will be set and followed. And we'll have an ethical organization and member's prosperity and success is guaranteed.

What is the goal of our company?

Have we accomplished all the goals we ever made?

Ask the Right Questions

Our mind has a very special ability which is critical to our attitudes: the ability to answer questions. No matter how ridiculous and unfounded our questions are, our mind can always find the answers to them.

Let's take a man who just lost his job and felt very depressed as an example. If we ask him questions like "What's wrong?" or what was the cause that made him lose his job, he could come up with a hundred negative responses and complains. Try asking the question, "Why am I not as successful as my spouse expects?" and we will get all kinds of preposterous responses. If we continue asking, we will continue answering. In contrast, if we ask positive questions like "What are the benefits of losing my job?" or "What responsibility should I be taking for this condition?" or "How can I help you?" attention will be focused on the responsibilities and solutions. Where our focus is and the attitude we have will influence our work, our life and everything. Therefore, we should have the awareness of asking the right questions. Always look on the bright side.

We could ask ourselves "How can I generate more business?" instead of "Why don't I have enough business?"

These are questions we suggest that can be used for generating our desired business.

1.What goals do we have for our business?

"Goals are dreams with deadlines"-by Zig Ziglar.

We need to have a clear picture of what we want to accomplish in a year, or five years. If we do not even know our own goals, how can others help us? It is like we want to travel abroad but we are not certain of our destination. How can the airline company agent sell us a ticket? Without goals, we won't have a predictable future.

2.What have we accomplished?

The consultant of my English school, always advises that we do two things. One is to write down our ideal situation and two, our accomplishments for the month.

Since we have an ideal for our success, we need to know how far away we are from our dreams. We have to have figures we can compare to then make better plans. That is the map for our success. We can direct ourselves and others to help reach our goals.

3. What are our advantages and what is our unique selling point for our products or services?

Can we explain the differences between our competitors and ourselves? What is our competitive strength? What is that "something" that others don't have, or the "something" we have that is superior to others? We need to be specific like laser spot lights. Figure out our competitive strengths then we can compete in value, not only in price. We can then introduce ourselves and our products or services more brilliantly to our friends and referral partners.

Also there are some wonderful questions we could ask to stay passionate at our work:

4. What kind of business makes me happy?

Focus on what we have instead of what we don't have.

Use this happiness as fuel for life and business.

5. What kind of business makes me excited?

We should always empower our victories and de-power our failures. Stay focused on things that excite us.

6. What kind of business will give me the feeling of itching to get on with it?

Take action!! Direct our intention to move and act.

7.Who are we grateful to in building our business?

When we start naming out the people who have assisted us in our career, we will be surprised at how lucky we are and that we know so many valuable people.

Positive attitudes will attract positive results. Ask ourselves these questions before we go to bed or when we get up. Or pair up with friends or members we trust, ask each other these questions. We will be surprised at the power of these questions. **Remember to ask the right questions and we will for sure start to expand and get a lot of referrals in business.**

Super Power Team

We wonder about the skills and correct ways to become successful all the time. Sometimes, it is much more confusing to figure out the answers than Alice in Wonderland. We spend a lot of time in our lives trying to learn through trial and error. However, we do not have all the time in the world to experience all the mistakes we could ever make, we need to have mentors and consultants in life to show us the correct direction and shorten our time for success.

My consultant, Stephen Wu tells us one of the most critical things for success is to surround ourselves with the right people. We need to select what platforms we are on and who our partners are.

For example, when two wolves come to the prairie, one might feel very upset for it does not see any meat. That's what we call "eye-sight". The other wolf is excited for it knows when there is grass there will be goats somewhere. We call that "vision".

Everyone has eyes, but not everyone has vision. Everyone has a brain, but not everyone has wisdom.

Take the plastic bag in the supermarket as another metaphor. If we put a cabbage in the plastic bag, then the price for the bag equals the price of a cabbage. If we put a lobster in the plastic bag, then the price for the bag equals the price of a lobster.

If we spend our time with monkeys in the jungle the best we can hope to be is "Tarzan". If we spend our time with wolves, we learn how to yelp and how to hunt.

Different platforms provide different values. Mingle with people with dreams and those who are motivated and driven. Mingle with excellent people then we will not become mediocre. Surrounding ourselves with diligent people, we will be hard working. Make friends with positive people and we will have no cause to complain.

The safest way to guarantee success is to surround ourselves with a SUPER POWER TEAM. We share the same goals of becoming successful in business and making more money through helping each other.

These are the requirements for a super power team:

S is for Support. People who support our goals and speak with candor when we make mistakes; they will be there when we need them.

U is for Understanding. We listen to each other's true heart. The deepest desire for people is to understand and to be understood. When we know that our communication is understood, we will open our hearts to them. Trust, respect and gratitude will grow.

P is for Prioritize. Noble entrepreneurs prioritize their schedules out of all the masses of messages and information. We select and put order into things we need to accomplish. We stay focused on the major tasks without wasting our energy.

E is for Ethics. We guard our personal integrity and honor our ethics. We do the right thing to benefit our business. We know that nothing is more important than to stick to our values and protect our reputation. People will judge whether to get closer to us or leave us by our reputation. Following true ethics will always bring good results. Also, the first thing immoral people lose is their freedom and their ability; they will become victims of their own crimes.

R is for Respect. We respect the differences of others. We know the shortcomings and advantages of every member in our team. Through respect we build better interpersonal relationships.

P is for persistence. We keep moving forward. We are never hindered by failures or obstacles. We know that success is about making the right decisions. And we keep on moving until we win. There is a Japanese saying, "If you have been knocked down seven times, then get up eight times." We are determined for success.

O is for originality. We create whatever is necessary. We do not complain about what we do not have, we innovate. We ask ourselves about "How can we make today better than yesterday?" "Where can we improve?" We train our minds and improve our abilities through originality.

W is for worth. We know the value of things we devote ourselves to. We recognize the values then we are motivated by them. We know the worth of helping others is not what we can get, but to know that we have the ability to help out.

E is for Enthusiasm. We love what we do and do what we love. True enthusiasm lies in the desire to prove ourselves and exceed ourselves.

R is for Responsibility. With or without titles or pay, we should all take the responsibility. What happens within our groups is what will happen to us. We consider everyone in our groups as extension of ourselves. We should all stop looking for excuses and be responsible for the result of our organization and our lives. Be the best we can be. The result of our organization is shaped by our decisions and actions.

Then we need a team to work with. The definition of a team is a combination of noble entrepreneurs gathered together to accomplish goals through cooperation and collaboration and sharing in experiences for success.

T is for Target. We are a group of people who share the same mission and vision and we act for the same purpose. We will follow the rules and regulations and the code of honor for our organization.

E is for Education. We will learn and correct our mistakes. We will practice our skills and learn to improve them. Through learning and training we gain new concepts to break our limitations. Limitations are set by our own false ideas. We educate ourselves to become true leaders and to be competent.

A is for ability. All of us need our best ability to accomplish the mission, just like the super heroes in The Avengers. Every one of us should contribute to each other and our team.

M is for mastery. Whatever we do, we hold the attitude to be the first, the best, the most and the only. We finish our mission and task to our utmost. As Steve Martin once said, **"Be so good they can't ignore you!"** We acquire mastery of our professions and we have no competition for we are way ahead of them.

If we multiply one one million times the result is still one. However, if we multiply 1.1 only seven times (1.1x1.1x1.1x1.1x1.1x 1.1x1.1=2.1435881) the sum is greater than two. If every member in our team provides ten percent more effort to helping each other and improves ten percent of their ability, picture how powerful that team that can be.

We are blessed to own a super power team of 42 members. The sum of multiplying 1.1 forty-two times is 54.763992375.

Create a super power team like this and we will not only be successful in life and business, we will be invincible.

Time

Our achievement depends on where and on what we spend our time.

If we spend our time drinking, we achieve our capacity for liquor.

If we spend our time complaining, we achieve a plaintive personality.

If we spend our time maintaining our face, we achieve beauty.

If we spend our time maintaining fitness, we achieve health.

If we spend time on being picky, we became harsh.

If we spend our time learning, we accumulate wisdom.

If we spend our time in being with family, we achieve parental love.

If we spend our time in improving ourselves, we realize our dreams.

If we spend time helping others in growing their business, we gain business.

If we spend time helping others to succeed, we become successful.

Time is neutral.

There is no right or wrong way to use our time. What matters are our choices and the results of our choice.

There is no right or wrong way, only in choosing what the results will be.

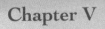

Chapter V

Referral Strategies

Chapter V
Referral Strategies

Interpersonal Relationship

In marketing strategies we establish product, place, promotion and price. However in networking, **"You build people and then people build the business."-Zig Ziglar.**

Almost everything we own in this world, we get through interpersonal relations. In this high-speed society, filling up with technology and competition, life is always changing. Most of us have forgotten that the most critical factors in success and business are our interpersonal relations and the connection between people. People tend to develop their relationships for the results they desire. However, the ironic fact is that the closer our relationship is with our team members and customers the more abundant the results are; and the faster and easier it is to generate and receive business. **We need to be very clear that the purpose of our lives is to help, to help ourselves and to help others. Our organization is a tool, a platform to help members to achieve their potentials and to help clients to realize their dreams. The purpose of our organization is to help members to make more money, not to make money for their own organizations.**

Furthermore, the interactions we have between people influences our happiness from the social aspect, as research by David Sirota, the author of The Enthusiastic Employee indicates. **Good interpersonal relations in the workplace are one of the three most critical elements that employees emphasize.** The other two are fairness and accomplishment. To many, dealing with the very complicated challenges of work is possible, but dealing with the relationships with our coworkers or colleagues is difficult. We feel our hands bound and we are unable to do anything about it.

Chinese people use particular methods to try to better understand people and control their futures. We use eight characters and study facial features and palm reading in order to gauge the personalities of people. However, the disadvantages of fortune telling are that we need to know birthdays and the times they were born, without which, results are inaccurate. People who are not familiar with us normally won't give us such detailed information. They will be suspicious. And in reading facial features, most females wear make-up and even worse, they might have had plastic surgery. These factors make it very difficult to gather useful information.

In Western culture, we have the horoscope and blood types but the same situation applies. How will strangers give us such private information?

Everything we own is through our interpersonal relations; therefore, in my World English School, we apply the nine Enneagrams of Interpersonal Relationships theory innovated and coached by Da-Shu Wu. Learning how to apply it made our business expand and have fewer personal problems by increasing our level of understanding about human nature and respecting others. **The common principle is "empathy". We don't need to flatter or accommodate. We understand the logic of their thoughts and respect the differences.**

There are differences between people; we have our own motivations and values. Different personalities should be managed with different methods. **There isn't any enneagram superior or inferior to another. Every type has its own benefits and disadvantages.** For example, a person who cares very much about rules and regulations, his advantage is to follow rules. However, his disadvantage is that he does everything according to rules. If the rules are not perfect, he will have internal contradictions and inconsistencies. For a person like me, we love to give help. However the disadvantage could be that we sometimes provide things others consider unnecessary and we feel hurt when others do not acknowledge us. **By understanding the traits of different people, we can connect with our teammates by using a common language and adopting more flexible management styles to arouse their strengths.** I used to observe this world with my own perspective and it seemed that I lived in my own universe. After knowing and applying this, I am able to expand my own universe to a wider range and connect with people in the remaining universes. By understanding others' characteristics and respecting their value,

Please respect
My tranquility

Please respect
My authority

Please respect
My rules

Please respect
My dream

Please respect
My devotion

Respect

by Coach Da-Shu

Please respect
My ways

Please respect
My achievement

Please respect
My thoughts

Please respect
Personal difference

we will know how to provide the assistance they really desire. We will for sure build a great and solid relationship and we will have endless business.

Be busy in providing service instead of being busy in exploiting business.

Motivational Competition

How wonderful it would be if we have a team and there is only cooperation without competition! However, is it really possible or is it just an ideal?

How can we manage an insurance company or real estate or any sales job service? Every worker in an insurance company sells the same products to their own customers and they have weekly sales competitions and monthly competitions all year round. If there is constructive competition, it is like setting a goal for workers and their attention will be on the goal then most workers won't have time to fool around.

The purpose of constructive competition is to help workers stay focused and to motivate them; even if there is an organization with members in different professions. Will there be a guarantee of business for every member? Is it a requirement that members only do and share their business with members within the organization?

For example, if we need an interior designer for our newly bought house. Do we give our case to our original interior designer who has delivered wonderful and satisfying service for years and with whom we have a wonderful relationship, or do we give it to the interior designer whose service quality we are not sure about, in our organization? This case might cost us US$1 million. Will we risk our money? The answer is obvious. Can we say this kind of competition is incorrect?

To build word of mouth for a team, we only need to continually demand high quality service. Only when we are willing to compete will we be willing to be compared.

It takes every member to agree upon:

- **Top quality**
- **Excellent service**
- **Can communicate and receive communication**
- **Be grateful**
- **Progress and improve for perfection**

Be self-disciplined

Do it first and don't justify for our members. Do not condone. Since we want to build a great reputation, we need to possess flawless and undefeatable ability and service quality. Review ourselves. Review our force of competition. Support of team members should be rational rather than emotional or we will damage the reputation and the credibility of ourselves in our team, and lose.

Some people think there shouldn't be too much interaction between different chapters, groups or organizations. The leaders worry that it will generate unnecessary negative effects. Actually if members obey and follow the code of honor and act ethically when they compete, then it is constructive competition. It is called cross-industry cooperation. Such interaction sometimes generates fireworks and might have ineffective results.

But constructive competition between team and team can be very motivating. It is the opportunity for them to learn the advantages from others and to improve, it inspires team progress and encourages them to strive to go beyond.

Competition is not necessarily a bad thing. Sometimes it is the motivation; as long as the leader sets the protective mechanism and rules of the games, the system naturally will come up with the solutions for mistakes. **If we are afraid to make mistakes, we will do things in the same old ways and we will always get the same mediocre results.**

Improvement comes from trial and error.

Constructive competition will provoke combat pursuit to win. Awards, medals and trophies are all there for encouragement.

Take constructive competition as a self-discipline principle and an accelerator for our organization to generate more business.

Tools, Resources, Support

There is a saying by Confucius, **"For a worker to do a perfect job, first he must sharpen his tools."**

To make a cup of tasty tea, we have to use proper tea sets.

To make mountain tea, we need clay pots.

To make flower tea, we need China. Without a proper tea set we can't experience the spirit of the tea.

To grow as a team, the team should have all the available tools.

We need to have platforms where we can interact and build meaningful relationships with people and generate business for each other. That's one of our tools. The organizations or groups we belong to are our major tools. Our mindset is another tool. Only by changing our minds can we change our actions and hence have different results.

If we join an organization with a mindset of consumers, we will focus on what we don't have. We will complain about not having the "correct brochures", "manuals", or "props". No support. No this... No that...

If we join our team with the mind of entrepreneurs, we will still notice what we don't have but instead of complaining, we solve the challenges. We make things happen.

Different mindsets result differently.

Other tools we could use are the website, the name tag or pin of our organization. These are for the overall degree of recognition and consistency.

Our teams are our brands. Cultivate them and make them become trademark brand names. We could also have songs, websites, promotional materials and uniforms for our teams to add value and to arouse topics to discuss. We wear the pins to show that we are proud of being part of our groups, to show our identity.

When all the tools are prepared, it is the moment to seek resources and support.

The resources are the circle of influences (people we know) behind our team members. **Never assume or underestimate anyone in our organizations.**

"You never know who they know."-Dr. Ivan Misner®, the Founder and Chief Visionary Officer for BNI®, the world's largest business networking organization

There was a classic story in my business networking chapter. We have a very talented architect. He is a regular award winner. He is very devoted in his own career and spent little time interacting with us. Everyone knows in our chapter that the father of the lady whose profession is the manager of ice-cream stores is a famous construction contractor. Her father owns a lot of land and is always looking for talented architects to cooperate with. It wasn't until I reminded him that he then realized that he nearly lost some great and ongoing business opportunities. Don't neglect the resources we have. We could be sitting on a diamond mine and we are totally unaware of it. Dig in and cultivate our resources. Then don't forget to support each other.

Resource is a noun. Without it, or if we don't use it properly, there will be no vitality.

To support is a verb, there won't be results if we don't act.

To give is to support.

To gain is to be supported.

To give is the release of one's resources; and to gain is to make the best use of our group resources.

Don't forget our most beneficial intention!

The Law of Reciprocity

"If you help enough people to become successful, you will eventually become successful." Dr. Ivan Misner®, the Founder and Chief Visionary Officer for BNI®, the world's largest business networking organization

It is a law that what we do to others comes back to us. Therefore there is a saying in Chinese, **"Good deeds attract good results. Bad deeds attract bad results."** So the philosophy of the world's largest networking organization is "Givers Gain®".

What is the best method for attracting business referrals? Definitely not through selling.

Dr. Ivan Misner®, the Founder and Chief Visionary Officer for BNI®, the world's largest business networking organization once said, "Remember everyone wants to buy but nobody wants to be sold." To Dr. Misner there are certain stages we need to go through. He called them Visibility, Credibility and Profitability, VCP®. People need to have a certain level of trust for them to give the money in their pockets to put in our pocket.

The fastest way to generate our trust and build a meaningful relationship is, in one critical word "help". Before others lend us their hands we need to be able to touch their hearts. Also, we should always take the initiative. We reach out to people rather than waiting for others to take action.

If we expect to get support then we should give our support first. If we wish to receive recognition then we should recognize others' efforts first. If we want to be respected, then we should respect others. Giving is the beginning of gaining.

Give our help first. Make appointments with symbiotic professionals, meet with them and understand their expertise and search in our circle of influence to see if there are any business opportunities we can connect them with. **Understand them thoroughly, know what their goals are for life and for business. Put in mind that the key word here is "help". Help with our hearts. Help without expectation for return. The best way to build a meaningful relationship is to assist our fellows to realize their goals.**

We have saved some gratitude in our social capital accounts. That will be our resource and social capital for future expenditure. One day when we need help, then it will come back to us. That is the law of nature-the law of reciprocity. The more help we provide the more social capital we can put in our accounts. We will become the richest business people in the world. I am pretty rich in this way. I have a lot of friends who I can call and they will lend me their hands without hesitation. I call them **"Sure Friends"**. They say yes immediately. How about you?

Also we can learn what their accomplishments are. We will get closer to them faster because people enjoy sharing their glories. We will find out what kind of people they are. If our member, Stanley has participated in a triathlon every year for ten consecutive years, we know he possesses strong willpower and we can trust him to persist. Sharing our accomplishments whether as students, workers, in the field of music, sports, arts or performance, we might find some surprises or similarities. At the same time our teammates will feel closer to us. **Do not forget to figure out where we can help them to accomplish more.**

The other aspects we should talk about are our interests and backgrounds. **The purpose of self-introduction is to get connected with others**-the school we went to, our blood type, etc.

We want to emerge with the feeling of "Wow, we have some things in common". People will naturally say "Me, too." I have a friend who is a lawyer and my general concept about lawyers is they are eloquent but not very easy to get close to. However, we were able to break the ice when we learned that we were born and grew up at the same place. We started to talk about our childhoods and that was the beginning of changing my impression about lawyers.

Try to find some areas that make us feel like we are in the same boat. In networking business, we build relationships with people through care and help first. Do not expect any quick benefits at first. It takes time to cultivate a true relationship.

Let our friends or members of the same organization feel our sincerity and our interest in learning more about them and helping them in some way. **I love the feeling of being able to help. The joy of seeing others become successful and realize their dreams is so precious.**

My consultant, Stephen Wu has made an excellent metaphor about the law of reciprocity. **He said the power of help is like when you push the water in the swimming pool, you push out with two hands in one direction and you will feel the power of the water coming back to you in the other directions surrounding you. It will come back and it will be stronger than your first push.**

What defines me is not the number in my back account. There will always be people who are wealthier and more successful than I am. However, I am pretty satisfied with the amount of savings I have in my social capital account. I truly believe the law of reciprocity. If I am not as successful as I desire, I will keep on helping and helping more and more and more until the whole universe returns me the favor. There is no such thing as failure to me. The only cause for failure is that I did not execute enough help and persist till the end.

Keep on helping and your business will come.

The Art of Chatting

The highest level of selling is the art of communication. We listen and we chat with our potential customers. Can we carry out a meaningful conversation?

True selling happens naturally, with very pleasant and enjoyable conversation. We discuss their wishes, worries and concerns. We chat about how to accomplish their goals and dispel their concerns and fears. There will not be any selling party or buying party in chatting. **True selling is when we sincerely want to help another solve the problems that bother them. There will not be any persuasion or pressure involved.** What we provide is the information or knowledge they want and need and will listen to. We provide meaningful and valuable services and products.

After the sale is done our customers appreciate us and they are grateful.

Many people consider selling a tough and stressful procedure. Once we learn the best way to sell, our feelings about selling will change. We used to think of selling as asking others to accept; therefore selling was a difficult test.

Now we need to reprogram our minds. Selling is a valuable and meaningful thing. Selling is helping others to realize their dreams and wave good-bye to worries. To make it simple—we help them to solve their problems.

True selling involves two steps:

1.To understand their wishes and worries wholeheartedly.

2.To apply our knowledge and provide our products or services to accomplish their dreams and eliminate their worries.

The greatest gain in selling does not lie in the rise of our sales figures, promotion to higher ranks, or the huge profits we can show off to our colleagues. The greatest gain in sales is our self-respect to our own purpose of life-to be able to provide people with positive help . The greatest gain in life is to have another person who trusts us in life.

Selling is the skill of chatting. It is the building of an interpersonal relationship. If we are not good at selling, it is only because we have not acquired the true art of chatting.

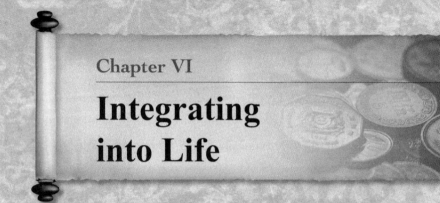

Chapter VI

Integrating
into Life

Your Contribution Lives On

Everyone has a position on the team or organization. How should we define our existence? Should we be unique, demand credit or show off to demonstrate our value? Are we only valuable when we defeat others? How should we consider our status on the team or in the organization?

I remember attending a training seminar held by BNI® Hong Kong in October, 2014. The guest speaker was Mr. Tom Fleming, the owner of more than 42 Platinum Chapters each with over 50 members in Florida. I was very excited to have the chance to shake hands with him. Mr. Fleming stood right next to the door greeting everyone. I walked up to him and shook his hand and said "Hi, Tom! Nice to meet you! I am Hsing-Hui. I am just a member." Tom patted me on my shoulder and said "You are more than a member." Later during the speech, he explained that the one thing he didn't like is when members say "I am just a member."

We underestimate our contribution and it seems that people who claimed they were just members tried to stay away from their obligations, wanted nothing to do with their own organizations.

What would happen if an orchestra member did not stay focused and played out of tune? The whole piece of music would no longer be harmonious and would become chaotic. One mistake could ruin the entire performance, couldn't it? There is no such thing as not being an important part.

Every one of us is as valuable as the others. We are all leaders without titles. The success of an organization depends on the creation of environments and cultures of contributing and taking the initiative. Every member promotes innovation, inspires teammates, embraces change and is responsible for success or failure.

Everyone should hold an aggressive and positive attitude and be determined to perform their best. As long as every person does that the organization he or she belongs to will flourish and prosper. They will not only effectively change and adjust with their environment, but also become the best in their industries. **Everyone possesses unlimited potential. We should be aware of our existence and use it to be valuable to our organizations; and our contributions will live on.** It's not something we need to show off.

Recognizing our own power and abilities, we can make a difference in our organizations, our societies, our countries, and then the world!!

Our contribution will live on.

Create a Platinum Chapter

On August 23rd 2012 Hsu, Hung joined a business networking organization with only 17 members-he was number 18. The biggest chapter for that organization in Taiwan at that time had more than 40 members and Hsu, Hung's chapter was way behind.

Hsu, Hung holds the belief that he would rather be the head of a chicken than the tail of a cow. Since he had participated on the team, he considered it his duty to grow the team because he wants to be surrounded with winners. With this concept in mind, Hsu, Hung started to invite guests regularly and with his enthusiasm, set a new record with ten guests in one meeting. This was a game, so he played it to win.

On January 15th 2013, Hsu, Hung's ChangHsing Chapter held their year-end banquet. Hsu, Hung was the host and the name of the banquet was Becoming a Platinum Chapter. The goal was to become a team with more than 50 members. One of our members asked him, "Can we leave the year blank? Otherwise we won't be able to use it next year. " Hsu, Hung replied "I promise we will accomplish the goal this year." That night, Hsu, Hung rekindled the passion of his teammates. There were 27 members in January and they spent only three months to become a chapter with 50 members. Subsequently, they reached Super Platinum with over 60 members and kept moving up to 74. **This miracle started to motivate other chapters to head for more than 50 members to also become Platinum chapters in the north region of Taipei.** This remarkable achievement belongs to all their members for it takes more than one person to change the world and they would not have had the result were it not for the consensus of every member working with a common purpose. **Their contributions have influenced all chapters of the organization in Taiwan. Now Platinum Chapters with more than 50 members are common. Why? Because one team showed that it could be done. If they could do it, we can too.** They made it possible for others to succeed and by setting a good example, and went from ordinary to outstanding. They were the first Platinum Chapter in Taiwan and having rewritten the story of their lives and accomplished greatness, they will naturally inspire others to rewrite their own stories and live their dreams.

When There is a Will, There is a Way

Do you have dreams? What do you do to realize your dreams? What price would you be willing to pay for your dreams?

There are 4 kinds of people:

1.People who work for their goals.

2.People who hesitate.

3.People who want to harvest without farming first.

4.people who sit and wait for it to happen.

Larry Hung, the Director of ChangZhan Chapter is one of the first kinds of people who go for their goals. When Larry visited the BNI® convention in Hong Kong in 2012, he made a decision to launch a platinum chapter at kick off. At that time there was no platinum chapter or any chapter which had met the standard for the Hall of Fame. Larry was daring and courageous. He was the first one to dream big.

In January 2013, he started a core meeting for ChangZhan Chapter with a group of five people at McDonald's. They were Ta-Ming Chang, Jun-Han Chen, Chung-Lin Wang, Hsin-Chieh Liu and Chun-Jung Lin.

Ta-Ming was our first chairman, Chun-Jung was the second chairman and Chung-Lin was the chairman of our third session. I was number eight to come on board for I was inspired by Larry's passion. We did not know we were shooting for a goal no-one else had reached before in Taiwan. The average number of members was under thirty. We were like bumblebees. Theoretically, it is impossible for bumblebees to fly for they have huge bodies and small wings. It violates the laws of physics. Bumblebees are able to fly because they cannot understand human language and so they do not know that they cannot. They fly because they want to. We were the same, we were driven by the vision Larry gave us without knowing how challenging it was.

However, we did have one advantage, we were able to follow the correct concepts and theories expressed by Dr. Ivan Misner®. I studied all the available documents, books and videos Dr. Misner had posted on YouTube. We had the best coach. As a result, there were two major elements that differed between us and all the existing chapters during that period, we made it fun and provided referrals passionately for each member.

We had the correct mindset originated by the founder of our organization. We made the decision to take up the responsibility and execute our goal with an all-out effort. We were earnest and accepted every challenge. We set up our high standard meeting room, greeted our visitors with our most welcoming visitor hosts and hostesses. We delivered the most professional meetings and kept them fun. All members wanted the dream to happen. As Norm Dominguez the Vice Chairman Emeritus for BNI®, the world's largest business networking organization, once told me "Faith makes it happen."

On July 2nd 2013 we kicked off the first platinum chapter with 51 members when launching and we were the first chapter with a lawyer, an accountant, an architect and a doctor as members. The legend goes on. We were awarded the fifth largest BNI® chapter in the world in 2014 and we were the biggest chapter in Taiwan with 80 members. We also won the award for the largest average referral amount for members at the 2015 convention in Taiwan. Once this record was broken, more and more chapters entered the Hall of Fame by becoming platinum chapters. It is no longer a "Mission Impossible".

I heard a story about Roger Bannister told by the founder of SeaBiscuit, Da-Shu Wu. For many, many years, people firmly believed that it was impossible to run one mile in less than four minutes. They thought that this feat was beyond the limitations of human beings. Even biologists confirmed that theory. Everyone accepted the "fact" except one—Roger Bannister. As a medical school student from England, Bannister set an astounding record by finishing one mile in 3 min 59.4 seconds on May 6 1954. He shattered the myth and established the legendary "miracle mile." However, his glory only lasted 46 days before it was broken again. Now there are literally hundreds of people who have finished running the mile in under four minutes, including high school students. When Roger Bannister broke the spell, other athletes could see the possibilities and their potential. He made others understand the fact that a new mindset brings about new results.

At the end of 2014, Tony Hsu led YongEn Chapter to become the first platinum chapter in Taoyuan. They also won an award for recruiting the most members in April and May in 2015. On May 22, Dalton Chang launched a new chapter and set a world record with the highest number of members. Xin-Du-Xin launched with 63 members with Doris Chang as the chairperson and Elli and Kevin Wu on the leader team. In two weeks, Kevin Yang broke Dalton's record. Kevin started his first core meeting for FuLe Chapter on November 4th, 2014. When FuLe Chapter was launched, there were 83 members. Larry Hung, Tony Hsu, Dalton Chang and Kevin Yang are all leaders with a visions.

Chung-Lin Wang, Chun-Jung Lin and Doris Chang are the leaders who support and direct the dreams. Hsing-Hui Huang and Kevin Wu have duplicated the spirit of education and training and deliver it to their chapters.

When there is a will, there is a way.

Discover 922

From March 27 to September 25, Hsu, Hung was the chairman of ChangHsing Chapter. He attended the Member's Success Programs during this period of time because he wanted to set an example in learning the rules and applying them; and through this to gain valuable organization experience, save time and become more effective.

September 22, 2014 was the last Member's Success Program before Hsu, Hung left his leadership team as the chairman and he volunteered to his executive director to be the guest speaker. He knew it would be his only chance to really show his results. The theme was Critical Moment-Why Should We Invite Guests?

Hsu, Hung had been the team leader and winner of two annual championships for the most introduced new members and the largest number of referrals, so he was not rejected. These results had been from competition rather than an election or choice, so were completely objective and ChangHsing had won with real strength.

Sharing in Hsu, Hung's success was an unforgettable and outstanding moment and **he gave a provocative and encouraging speech.**

That was the first time the two leading chapters in Taiwan,

ChangZhan and ChangHsing had come together. There was constructive competition hidden within the jocular admiration and humor.

After this meeting, Hsing-hui Huang went to visit Hsu, Hung at his essential oil company and together they decided to cooperate to write a book recording the spirit of noble entrepreneurs. Furthermore this special book would be released in both Chinese and English at the same time by the two Taiwanese writers. It was the first time ever in the book publishing history of Taiwan that we would have a Chinese book published with an English translation in firm and confident form. They set their goal of showing the spirit of Taiwanese business people to the world.

Their friends responded immediately and they soon gathered more than thirty partners to support this book. The process was not as smooth as they had expected, but since they firmly trusted each other a kinship quickly formed.

Finally, the two made a decision to gather the 42 Noble Entrepreneurs inspired by "Buddha Chapter 42".

They met on 9/22, and completed most of the interviews and written articles within 4 months which was in accordance with their goal setting.

Without the encounter of 9/22, there could never have been the existence of this book. Thanks to the discovery of 9/22.

42 Chapters Written with Spirit

A sutra of forty two chapters has been discussed many times in Chinese history and has even been portrayed in films.

It is said that it was the first translated Buddhist scripture brought from India to China. It was a combination of the words from Buddha Sakyamuni.

The books "Big in Business" written in both Chinese and English have gathered the success stories of 42 Noble Entrepreneurs. They are positive stories of the process of fighting against adversity and taking risks to become successful.

Some were born lucky, some were unfortunate, some were born with a mission to accomplish, some needed to struggle, some rose after falling and others became legends. Their persistence and intelligence are a reference for others who are searching for success.

After we finish reading the mindset and attitudes of these noble entrepreneurs, we will ask ourselves: "What are our excuses for quitting? What are our excuses for not making it?" If we could make it happen, what is there to stop us?

When travelling as a tourist what we see is sometimes scenery after packaging. We might not be able to sense the true culture or customs of the country.

When we meet a person for the first time, our first impression is usually masked by social etiquettes. We can rarely glimpse the true sincerity of the person.

These 42 Noble Entrepreneurs might not be the successful business people the media reports about. However, they are motivational and inspiring. They have used their true lifetime experiences to make the best of themselves. They are not defined by the amount of money in their bank accounts. Instead, they define themselves by the amount of help they give to society.

Although we do not come from people who are born rich and have strong backgrounds, we still have mutual admiration. We might not own powerful social capital, but we have team morale.

What glues us together is **the heart of our social responsibility for a better Taiwan and our mutual vision to change the world's point of view about business people.**

Ride on with us!

The 42 Common Traits of Noble Entrepreneurs

1. Motivation:

Noble entrepreneurs have a strong burning desire for success. We encourage ourselves when others don't.

2. Guts:

We dream big and adventure bigger.

Noble entrepreneurs accomplish impossible missions and there is no such thing as failure in our dictionaries. We conquer. We are unique and we don't worry about others' judgments our comments about our temporary failures.

3. We set goals and accomplish them:

We know what we want. Targets help us to stay focused. We are productive every day. Having goals will provide us the energy. It will be the Polaris to lead us out of the darkness to live colorful lives.

4. Knowledge:

Noble entrepreneurs continue to accumulate knowledge all our lives. Knowledge is power. A day doesn't go by without learning something. We learn to better ourselves.

5. Honesty:

Noble entrepreneurs are straightforward, frank and honest. We put ethics into our business and daily life. We don't lie for the benefit of business.

6. Positive postulates:

Noble entrepreneurs never doubt about becoming successful. We stay focused on the upcoming good. We firmly believe "It's going to happen just like that." We work toward accomplishing our postulates.

7. Flexibility:

Noble entrepreneurs try to verify the truth before we judge. We ask the resources for information. We will evaluate things fairly with open minds. We admit we can be wrong and are willing to change our thoughts accordingly.

8. Passion:

We love what we do. We do what we love.

9. Dare to risk:

We overcome our fear of failure. We know we can learn from books and others' experiences and then always make the right decisions from our mistakes.

10. Energetic:

Noble entrepreneurs don't sit and wait. We are determined to make it happen. We know it is not our ability that determines our destinies. It's our decision to make it happen. Determine our destiny.

11. Initiative:

Noble entrepreneurs look for opportunities. We are not afraid of trying the unknown.

12. Convincing:

Noble entrepreneurs know how to motivate others. We believe in what we do. We know how to encourage and inspire others to follow our dreams.

13. Outgoing:

Noble entrepreneurs are easy going and make friends easily. We are willing to help and have many valuable friends.

14. The ability to communicate:

Noble entrepreneurs effectively deliver our thoughts to others and are willing to receive communication as well. We are simple, honest and inspiring communicators. We speak the truth with respect.

15. Patience:

Noble entrepreneurs are patient to others. We understand not everyone owns the ability we have. We are patient in explaining and willing to wait. We know that what makes wine and vinegar different is time.

16. Perfection:

Noble entrepreneurs do not accept mediocre. We hold high standards and always strive for the best. We are the best we can be every single day.

17. Sense of humanity:

Noble entrepreneurs laugh at our mistakes. We don't feel offended when we face teasing. We have fun all the way to success. Having fun increases our effectiveness.

18. Versatility:

We are talented. We are good at sports, dancing, music, art, etc. we enjoy our lives and admire the beauty in them.

19. Curiosity:

We are not afraid to admit we do not know something. We ask questions of the experts. We are interested in all the things around us.

20. Adaptability:

We enable ourselves to adapt to a fast changing environment. We are willing to consider new options and make adjustments.

21. Honor:

We believe in our own codes of honor and do what is right. We are not hindered by objections or obstacles.

22. Benefit others:

We plan ahead and think big. We are committed to accomplishing great things. We not only think of ourselves, but also for the good of others.

23. Imagination:

Noble entrepreneurs use our imagination to envision facts. We create our own universe through imagination and by doing the same things from different points of view. Those great inventions start from the pictures in our minds.

24. Action:

Once we have dreams, we get on our horses and move forward. Action always speaks louder than words.

25. Persistence:

One of our mottoes is "Winners never quit. Quitters never win." We keep moving forward. We don't quit until we win.

26. Completion:

Noble entrepreneurs have the ability to finish every test. We do not leave any mission uncompleted. We can start a process and finish our actions.

27. Focus:

Noble entrepreneurs stay focused on the strong points rather than the defects. This makes us concentrate on our goals. We are like horses with blindfolds that go straight forward to accomplishing results.

28. Results:

Don't cheat about the results. We don't listen or make excuses or complain. We evaluate with results in minds.

29. Authenticity:

What is real to the noble entrepreneurs is real. We do not bother about other's opinions. We listen to the voice from our hearts.

As Dr. Seuss once said, "Be who you are and say what you feel, because those who mind don't matter and those who matter don't mind."

30. Innovation:

Noble entrepreneurs invent and create. We don't stick to past patterns. We stand from the point of view of our customers and make today better than yesterday.

31. Kudos:

Noble entrepreneurs inspire and encourage others. We admire others and cheer for others' hard work. We choose to only see the bright side of things. We applaud when they are "right" and we recognize others' superiority and praise their masterly performances.

32. Walk the talk:

Set an example. Doing it ourselves is the best way to influence others for positive change. No one likes to be forced. People will feel that you are depriving their freedom. However, if we show them a realizable example, they will be inspired and join us willingly.

33. Humble:

Only the humble can be great entrepreneurs. Isaac Newton said: "If I have seen a little further, it is by standing on the shoulders of giants."

All the noble entrepreneurs attribute our success to the cooperation of all the members of the organization. We cherish every member in our team.

34. Helpfulness:

Noble entrepreneurs are always willing to devote more and give beyond expectation. Helpfulness is part of our DNA. We believe in the law of reciprocity.

35. Nature:

Unselfish and do not care only about profit. Noble entrepreneurs take care of the relationships between their workers and customers. We nourish the relationship and treat all people with integrity and sincerity. We cultivate our reputation.

36. Exercise:

Exercise our bodies in order to achieve outstanding performance. Exercise can raise the function of our brains and our energy to effectively manage stress and extend our duration at work.

37. Leadership:

With or without titles, we lead. We take up the responsibility for the success of our companies and organizations. We earnestly act in our roles and create environments and cultures of every single person as leaders. We lead ourselves.

38. Introspection:

Noble entrepreneurs know that our lives are the outcome of our thoughts. Our lives are shaped by our decisions and actions. Therefore, noble entrepreneurs spend time to be introspective about our values, delete the barriers in our minds and reorganize our thoughts. We plan, revise our visions and program our futures.

39. Nutrition:

"You are what you eat." The food we eat will influence our performance. We form diet habits of winners. These keep our energy level at peak and provide a great mood.

40. Forgiveness:

Noble entrepreneurs forgive those who need to be forgiven. We do not bring harm or betrayal into our work places. We leave hatred behind. If we sink into the sorrows of our past, we move forward and are able to create extraordinary and wonderful futures. Only those burdened with pain will hurt others.

41. Gratitude:

Noble entrepreneurs are grateful for all the happiness and luck in our lives. Anxiety and gratitude cannot exist at the same time. We are thankful for all the wonderful things we encounter in life.

42. Cherish Family:

Happy families are our backup for hard work. We cherish and care about our family. We know the meaning of money is to make our families enjoy better lifestyles. We arrange our schedules and spend our time with our family.

Chapter Ⅶ

42 Taiwanese noble
entrepreneurs' inspiring stories

"That some achieve great success is proof to all
that others can achieve it as well"

~ Abraham Lincoln.
(Arranged in strokes of Chinese characters)

The Eco-Soldier
Min-Ying Fang（方敏穎）

Keelung, the City of Rain, has many good qualities but not all are as satisfying as they could be. The high rate of divorce, suicide and unemployment are an unwanted burden for Keelung residents. Although the abundance of rain makes the city and its countryside a perfect place for tea agriculture, the problems caused by air pollution make the city blue and grey. Even the honored guest that once visited the port, Rubber Duck could not escape its fate-it turned black from the soot and later self-detonated.

Min-Ying is no exception as a typical resident of Keelung. She has been the shy, silent type since as long as she can remember but she has often led herself into challenges which have brought her a whole world of surprises, adventures and, sometimes, conflicts.

During her high school years, Min-Ying entered the school table tennis team and played for her school in the Republic of China National Games. Later she studied at the Department of Environmental Engineering and Science of Feng Chia University. She also leaded her table tennis team as a captain to won the honor of first four ranks for four consecutive years. There she gained knowledge of ecology and developed a deep understanding of environmental protection.

After graduation, she worked as a salesperson for several pharmaceutical companies and was responsible for the sale of a cholesterol lowering drug for ten years.

During those years, Min-Ying won the trust of her clients and doctors with her diligence and sincere attitude. Meanwhile, she managed to accomplish her sales goals without creating pressure for her clients. She even joined the "million-income" club with her yearly income averaging 1.8 million TWD (60,000 USD) and in her best she year reached 2.28 million! She had reached the level of a super salesperson, but just when she arrived at this new plateau, Min-Ying suddenly left the company because she had become tired of the culture of the pharmaceutical industry and was no longer able to feel passion for her work.

While her many colleagues were still in shock from her decision, Min-Ying was aboard a flight to Boston to begin studying her Master's Degree in Business Administration at the famous Hult International Business School. Furthermore, she was to finish the program in only one year and received many offers from local US companies to stay and work for them. However, Min-Ying chose to return to Taiwan, not out of any dislike for the US, but because she terribly missed her home and family.

Min-Ying wants to express her appreciation to Teresa Wu,

who always lends out her hands with a smile on her face. She has outstanding family background but stays humble all the time. She was her classmate in graduate school. She provided Min-Ying was at the valley of her life. Min-Ying wants to say "Thank you Teresa! You are one of my best friends!"

In September 2009, Min-Ying returned to Taiwan to advance her plans for the future, but she soon discovered that her parents were unhappy with her decisions and unable to come to grips with the paths she was choosing. She knew that her parents were just worried about her; about whether she had made the correct decisions and whether she was drawing the wrong blueprint for her life. But she just couldn't help feeling upset about it. And there was blame and recriminations.

They couldn't understand why their daughter had given up a million-dollar yearly income to spend three million dollars on a master's degree that she would never use. They also couldn't understand why she had wasted her youth in a relationship that she later abandoned. But most importantly, they couldn't understand why she was choosing a path full of risk and uncertainty instead of settling into a secure, lifelong career.

After withstanding her parents' impassioned reproach, Min-Ying jumped into her car and went speeding down the highway. She held tight to the wheel as she held tight to her dreams, but still the tears dropped from her eyes like rivulets of salty rain.

Min-Ying said "Although I have benefit in the medicine industry. Being a salesperson the outstanding performance in selling medicine provides me the money to study abroad and investment fund. I am neither a physician nor a professional authority. I know that drugs should be the final means for maintaining health. The medicine used to control diseases burdens our liver and kidney and leaves immediate or long term side effects. Also the disposed unused medicine causes pollutions in the environment it become part of environmental hormone. And later comes back to our bodies through water or soil. We actually use four elements like balanced diet, regular exercise, adequate sleep, pleasant mindset to maintain our health. However, most people are too busy or too ignorant to use these concepts achieve our goal of healthy body. I have long searching for great products to help people to regain or main our health. Fortunately I find a whole series of products that assist people to sleep better and restore our physical mental strength. And also replace their stress with pleasant mind. They can also boast the immune system and raise our metabolism. My mission is to protect the environment for destroyed by human beings from the damage of drug abuse."

On the other hand, the haze is one of the main factors that destroys our health. Min-Ying knows the quality of fresh air is very critical. The promotion of purified air is her other focus.

Five years have flown by. During this time Min-Ying has been studying and working on developing a high quality air-purifier for the energy, medical and nanotech industries; a device which could counter the effects of man-made environmental pollution and reduce the harm of drug abuse.

Although her income is no longer as copious as it had been, Min-Ying feels more comfortable and at ease with herself. For money is not the grand pursuit of her life, but to make what she does meaningful and worthwhile while creating benefits for others and for herself.

Changing careers can be difficult, harsh, full of pressure and sometimes lonely because others will never understand what they have never experienced. Hard as it was, Min-Ying has never forgotten that she graduated with the knowledge of environmental science and therefore is carrying her mission to promote environmental protection and awareness.

In 2014, Min-Ying joined a business network organization where she found associates who could share her dreams and give her a sense of belonging. They now support each other, working together and are quickly making progress towards their ideals.

Min-Ying still believes that her hard work will eventually yield fruit and she will reach her goal of creating a balance between development and environmental preservation. One day, her achievements will make her parents satisfied and relieved.

She appreciates the support that she's received so far and everything that has happened in her life-no matter whether good or bad. Most of all, she's proud of herself for not giving up and holding on to her dreams.

The Sea Prince who takes care of everything
Chung-Lin Wang（王崇霖）

Living a life on the stormy waves builds character and self-esteem. Life is like the tide-it comes and goes, and like the waves there are many ups and downs. Thrown into deep water there are several choices: some give up and drown, some panic and others just drift with the waves. But some fight furiously for survival. The light on the lighthouse shore is always burning brightly. It is really up to the helmsman to sail toward or away. This is the poignant story of a tough teenager from Keelung.

Chung Lin was born into a merchant family. He could always smell fish, even in his dreams. They owned a small store (Wan Mei Xiang) on Ai 3rd Rd in Keelung. The store sold many kinds of seafood and breads. It was one of the most popular gathering spots in the neighborhood.

Their house would often be crowded with celebrities and famous people. Even the mayor of Keelung would be a guest during holidays and festivals. This gave Chung Lin a sense of importance and superiority and he lived a happy childhood of nice clothes and entertainment. One night, when Chung Lin was in the 7th grade and their house was packed with a large crowd, news reached his family that his father had been imprisoned for smuggling to the mainland (China). Everyone in his family was anxious. In the following months, his grandfather spent almost all their family's wealth to release his father from prison. From then on, Chung Lin's life sank from being a sea-prince in a golden palace to being a slave in an undersea abyss. They moved from their mansion to a cabin in the suburbs.

Their entrance into the world outside shifted from a luxurious gate to a plain wooden back door. He had to transfer from his school for aristocratic children to a public junior high school. And his personality changed from one of great pride to utter abasement. Now he had to worry about the registration fees for public school. He was living a nightmare which constantly haunted his mind.

Chung Lin life was much different than before. He set up a small stall at a local market selling beverages. He was timid and shy at first, but he knew what it would take to survive and so forced himself to shout out loud in order to sell his goods. He shouted from morning to night and over the weeks his skin turned from white to dark. He was the "little dark" shuttling beverages in the markets of Keelung.

We-Ya (the annual year-end dinner when employers treat their employees for their dedication and hard work) fell on the same day as his birthday. On this day, his mother gave him a plump white bread wrapped in pork fat and pickled cabbage with sweet peanut powder sprinkled on top and wished him a "Happy Birthday." That was his one beautiful memory from junior high school.

His family had become so destitute that Chung Lin didn't dare to trouble his mother about tuition fees until the last day and his mother took him to their relatives to ask them for money. They scraped together enough money and his heart pounded with the desire for success. Chung Lin pledged in his heart that he would study and work hard to end this family tragedy.

Their family situation continued to worsen until they couldn't afford to pay their rent and they had to move to a cheaper area in Sanchung. Chung Lin lived at his auntie's house with his cousin who was four months younger. Although they were close, there were still many times when they quarreled together. Because of his family's situation he didn't dare to fight or talk back and he learned to stop expressing his own opinions and feelings. Nothing and no-one could enter his heart from then on. His heart for expression became closed. He transferred to an experimental class at the first boy's high school in HsinChu. He was away from his mother again and he wanted to save the fare on buses so he seldom went home.

He stayed at school and declined all invitations to visit friends' homes for meals because he didn't want to face their questions about his family situation. He had installed a screen from family life and he kept himself far away from it.

An advisor at Chung Lin's school would persuade him to come to their home to eat using the excuse of helping in his school work. This opportunity provided Chung Lin not only better nutrition but also a much-needed boost to his self-esteem. Finally Chung Lin began to feel there was a warm corner in the human world.

Under the influence of his teachers, Chung Lin double majored in Psychology and Business Administration at Fu Jen University. He became very active at school. He participated in the Acupuncture and Movie Clubs, he was a representative for public relations and was elected as representative for the school. He also modeled for the students at the Department of Textiles and Clothing. When he was out of class, he worked part time as a private tutor. In order to make money, save money and survive he took on a very demanding but high-paying job as a laborer doing such work as tying steel bars, carrying heavy bags of cement and moving furniture.

When he was in his third year, he qualified to be an exchange student with Stanford University in California. This experience enriched and expanded his horizons and while such experiences are usually easy and pleasant for most college students, Chung Lin continued to choose to pave his future with hard and earnest work. He gradually conquered his fears and began raising his own level of confidence. During his last year in college, he founded his own after-school class with two English teachers in Tucheng. They designed their own fliers and visited prospects door to door. In doing this, he not only provided opportunities for himself but his parents as well. This was the beginning of his life as an entrepreneur. After he finished military service, he worked at GM for nine years. He thought he might spend his entire career working in this company and looked forward to getting promoted and retiring with security.

However, he found a new direction for his life after listening to a speech given by Morris Chang. Morris said, "Young people need to choose professions that will contribute to society. By doing virtuous deeds these will reciprocate back to you. Your job will become your career and you will devote yourself to your career passionately and your career will become your inspiration." This speech was sobering and encouraging to Chung Lin and the giant within was awakened and from then on, he engaged himself in the insurance business.

"To make life better and more beautiful," is Chung Lin's vision for the insurance business. He now carefully develops insurance plans for his friends and relatives through sound actuarial principals in order to defend against such tragedies as ruined his childhood from happening to others. To limit the consequences of illness or accidents the odds are that a beautiful and wonderful life will eventuate. In addition to expertise and passion, Chung Lin possesses an infectious enthusiasm. He has won the favor of many celebrities who have allowed Chung Lin to develop their life insurance plans and provide financial planning and risk management. It's a hard-won trust and he cherishes this kind of credibility. Chung Lin has never forgotten the helpless and hopeless experiences that beset his childhood and youth in Keelung. In his life he has experienced many blessings. The sufferings and distress of his teenage years have served to give him a new lease on life. For all the salty and fishy smells of his childhood, there is a record of bravery and resilience, fighting against many unforeseen difficulties. For, like Triton, he has has arisen from the sea to spread his message of inspiration and help to the world.

The Practice and Development of Entrepreneurs
The grateful Business Consultant
Cheng-Hung Wu (吳政宏)

In 1963, Cheng-Hung founded China Agricultural Machines at the age of 23. His work involved operating agricultural tillers, machine maintenance and selling machine parts. He started an agricultural revolution in Yi Lan in northeast Taiwan. He rode his motorbike everywhere promoting his revolutionary concepts of using machines to replace human labor. He contacted every farmer in the entire area, never giving up until he had tracked them all down and made his concepts known. He knew that farming was a laborious job and that life for a farmer is tough. But doing business as a descendant of a strict family which didn't drink or smoke and who wasn't good at social intercourse was even tougher.

Soon, however Cheng-Hung's competitors began to cut their prices in order to stay in business and he wasn't smart in choosing employees so was cheated again and again. There were bad debts and bad checks he couldn't cash from his clients.Bad turned to worse when one of his friends wouldn't return money he had loaned to him and one of his employees stole his money. There was one disaster after another. By this point, Cheng-Hung was ready to quit but his mentor, Songling Zen advised him carefully and patiently and gave him precision guidance. He suggested that Cheng-Hung try implementing two integrated methods:

1. Insist on a fixed price but teach maintenance skills for free as added value.

2. Pay cash immediately when purchasing parts from suppliers.

These two seemingly simple ideas were an immediate and effective strategy for the situation. The clouds dissipated and life was restored to his business. His implementation of honesty and integrity in doing business gave him credit and his business was able to expand gradually through word of mouth. He hired five excellent employees, one of whom opened his own business five years later.

Doing business is to be earnest not crafty and fawning.

His most impressive lesson came from news that a competitor in the same trade now owed money more than US$66,000 from a loan. Cheng-Hung realized the importance of having a business consultant. The person on the ground is sometimes baffled by problems and only an onlooker, who can see more of the game, can see the answer clearly.

Cheng-Hung was thirty years old and he vowed that he would devote the rest of his life to being a corporate consultant with the conscience to learn and help business owners to succeed so that society could prosper and people could live happy, healthy lives. Once he made the decision, he retired from China Agricultural Machines and passed it on to his business partners who had been running the company with him. Their company is still running very well today. Here was an example of Cheng-Hung's generosity.

At the very beginning of his career as a consultant his first cases were extremely successful. But soon he reached a dilemma. The business had to decide whether or not to lower the prices of their product. If they did, the financial manager claimed the product line would be unsuccessful. The sales manager and the financial manager debated until the financial manager asserted that "the more business we do the more money we will lose." The general manager was overwhelmed by the situation and asked for Cheng-Hung's advice. Cheng-Hung responded, "More haste, less speed! Let's decide tomorrow."

He then went to his own advisor for suggestions. Songling advised that "different industries should use different strategies so do not generalize every industry. As long as a company continues to operate, there will always be a chance of success." Ah! That's the way it is. Count on back-up experts. Then you won't fail under any circumstances. You will have a guarantee of success.

In the second year of his consulting business, Cheng-Hung faced a further challenge which was to be critical to his company's survival. Hong asked for help from a professor named Chen Yi-An who pointed out the right path to him. He said, "Life is beautiful. All is the best for me. It's okay to make mistakes. Just don't make the same mistake twice."

Cheng-Hung then looked into his business strategy and found the mistake. They were spending too much energy trying to cultivate their own consultants in order to reduce costs and the people they trained were not experts in the field. They weren't able to give effective advice and therefore they weren't accumulating enough satisfied customers or creating good "word of mouth". Cheng-Hung repented and corrected his faults. He appointed himself as the president and started to hire the best consultants he could find and strengthened their performance. They become so well known that demand skyrocketed. Consequently, they bought a new office the following year. The right strategy resulted in high achievement. Cheng-Hung is grateful for the instruction and inspiration of his two mentors.

The Qun-Ying Mastermind Consulting Co., Ltd. has been smoothly and successfully consulting business enterprises for more than 30 years.

If those business owners had had more knowledge and practice in business management they could have run their businesses in a much more relaxed and pleasant atmosphere and with a lot less frustration and unhappiness. Consultant Cheng-Hung possesses the spirit of a great businessman in assisting entrepreneurs to learn and practice the wisdom to identify people and their skills and to make the right decisions. His lifetime goal is to improve the entire management system in their industry and he hopes that all industries in Taiwan, whether big or small can become better, more productive and successful.

Locomotive
The creator of literature and art work
Hsien-Hung Wu（吳獻宏）

Experts see but laymen watch.

In his forty something years of life, Kevin (Hsien-Hung) has spent equal time in the south and north of Taiwan. Ten years in Hsinchu, ten years in Kaohsiung, ten years in Tainan and after getting married, twelve years in Luchou, New Taipei City.

He went to elementary school in Hsinchu until the fifth grade. During middle school he was in Lin-yuan, Kaohsiung. For his junior college five-year program he was in the Nan Jeon University of Science and Technology Electronics Department. Why Nan Jeon? Because it was furthest from home!

His family runs an iron factory and the bitter fumes and deafening environment made him want to get as far away as possible to focus on study.

However, his sense of responsibility made him learn first-hand the details of working and managing the factory and he gained the necessary certificates for operating it. Without teacher Kevin yet mastered the essential knowledge and dared to make use of it. That's why he is like a locomotive; devoting himself to helping people achieve their dreams.

Kevin's father's business was expanding so they bought another 800 pin of land and built three huge factories. But when his father suddenly died of lung cancer, Kevin was forced to take over the burden of repaying the loans for many years. He eventually paid back the debts, but he also had to close down the factories.

However, Kevin is thankful to his father for giving him the courage to reach his goals, no matter what. He always pushes himself to reach every goal he sets. This was the formation of Kevin's personal quality of a locomotive rushing ahead.

Kevin later started managing a wrapping company specializing in the customizing of gifts. Kevin has a hand in all the detailed plans of the business. He knows all elements must be coordinated and operate smoothly together.

He has learned all the needed skills to make it easier to lead and manage so his staff follows his experience and knowledge. Kevin learned 3D drawing, first to be able to communicate professionally with graphic editors and engineers. So long as each of his partners understand their own duties, it is much easier to put everyone in their positions of expertise to do their jobs properly.

Kevin also enjoys being a pioneer, doing different but meaningful things that no-one else has thought about or done before. It is in

Kevin's nature to create a customized product according to each customer's character and style, making it possible to stand out in the gift market.

With his past hardworking experiences, Kevin has long contemplated corporate structure. He has joined many societies hoping to discover a teamwork model with which to create a better future.

Kevin sees his group and society as his own company business, wishing to bring greatness to other people rather than just his own. His level of thinking and action has made him a popular figure everywhere he goes.

Kevin says, "There are many people who wish to see Taiwan succeed, but there are many more people watching than seeing."

The Fortune Keeper
Genie Accountant
Meng-Yen (Novia) Lee (李孟燕)

When operating in the business world, one role that is easily neglected but is actually critical is the accountant. A company depends on their accountant to operate legally. In Taiwan, according to general accounting principles, accountants are not allowed to promote themselves or advertise. Therefore, most of their business comes from word of mouth. To be able to provide high quality service and gain the trust of their clients is the highest guiding principle.

Having been a business man for many years, the number of accountants I've known are too numerous to detail. Novia (Meng-Yen) Lee is the one who impressed me the most. You won't smell money or see dollar signs in her eyes when you are around her. You will only see her gratitude and expectations. There have been three turning points in life which determined the success of her career.

The first turning point for Novia was when she accidentally entered the field of accounting. Novia's major at National Chengchi University was sociology. Usually students graduating from this department become civil servants or social workers. It is not easy to find another decent or relevant position. So Novia decided she had to look for another major. Accordingly, there was only one other department that matched her qualifications which wouldn't require her to take an oral exam. Under these circumstances, Novia earned her second major degree. There are no other explanations for **Novia's success than her determination and self-confidence.**

Novia's second turning point was rebooting her studies and becoming an accountant. After she received her master's degree in accounting at National Chung Chang University, she gradually earned fame and distinction for her hard work in the challenging working environment of KPMG Taiwan. Her devotion to her job was exemplified by her extreme working hours often working so late that her only friends were the lights of Taipei 101 ! It was a little too much for Novia and she left KPMG to find a totally different job at a biotechnology company. She enjoyed the regular working hours at first. Unfortunately, the company's business became worse and worse and eventually, Novia found herself idle almost every day with nothing better to do than to watch popular dramas. The only two things that moved were her thumb and eyes.

Then one day she had lunch with one of her very respectable friends who advised her to pick up her books to take the challenge to become a certified accountant. Novia willed herself to study again and with arduous effort she earned her CPA qualifications in one year. It was an incredible mission but Novia accomplished it because she knew the art of listening to precious advice and setting her **goals and** direction.

The third turning point was the establishment of her own accounting firm. One day Novia received a very unique request for a job interview requiring a licensed accountant who was willing to set up an accounting firm immediately. Novia replied to the request and went to the scheduled appointment. The interviewer was in charge of an investment consulting company. He worked closely with accountants in the services he provided but he was concerned with paying so many service charges to his accountants. So why not set one up himself? By doing so they could share their resources and reciprocate each other. The interviewer had looked through the data on human resources websites like 104 for qualified personnel and sent out invitations for job interviews. During the interview, he told Novia the first assignment was for her to set up a firm and he would be responsible for the expenses. It was like a job from heaven. Novia not only got her own salary but she could also develop her own business according to her performance without interference, so long as she could provide perfect service to all their clients. What an out of the world job offer! The only other task was to provide a one-page proposal of **how to establish her accounting firm.**

Though Novia had never thought about being her own boss, she is the kind person who keeps her word. So she sent back her earnest proposal in no time. So it went that Novia got the offer after her second interview and became the president of her own accounting firm. Later, Novia learned that at least twenty other accountants had been interviewed but none of them replied with their assignments. For the other accountants were far too good at calculating so they couldn't believe in such a good offer and none of them wanted to waste their time. Novia never calculates or evaluates matters with only numbers. All she cares is whether she can help and keep her commitments to family, friends, clients and those around her. Today Genie Joint CPA Firm is a firm with five accountants.

When dew descends from heaven, are you prepared with container in hands? Novia has performed diligently at every single stage of her life and encountered every desire and fortune of her dreams. However, what is fortune?

Fortune can be defined as: When a disaster hits I am not around. When an opportunity knocks I am prepared.

Novia is always ready for success. She has her feet firmly planted on the ground and knows there is no elevator to success; that you have to take the stairs.

People who value others gain value from others. What kind of accountant do you need for managing your enterprise? One who can bring you good fortune is the fortune accountant - Novia Lee.

Due to desired, she strives.

Due to belief, she pursues.

Due to her goal, she fights.

Due to clear directions, she persists.

Due to gratitude, she attracts luck.

Due to her help. she meets wonderful advisors.

Due to her investments, she harvests.

Steady and Serious Carpenter
Non-exaggerated
Min-Lang Ho（何敏郎）

Confucius said, "Shall I tell you what true knowledge is? When you know, to know that you know, and when you do not know, to know that you do not know—that is true knowledge." There are many explanations given by scholars, but no matter the interpretation all are very suitable to describe the character of A-Lang (Min-Lang). A-Lang's life is defined by sincerity and that is the attitude he holds when facing knowledge; the belief in intellectual honesty. A-Lang comes from a family of carpenters beginning with his grandfather. He is the third generation in the interior carpentry industry. When A-Lang was twelve, his father became very sick and had to receive dialysis treatment every day. The burden of supporting the family fell on his mother and she had to work at a factory during the day and would take care of his father at night. In order to reduce his mother's heavy load and financial burden, A-Lang and his three brothers worked from the time they were in junior high school. His father passed away when A-Lang was 25 and he became determined to find solutions without medicine or doctors.

He devoted his spare time to looking for answers in religion and folk remedies including Qigong and Tui Na (a form of Chinese manual therapy). A-Lang loves reading The Analects of Confucius and one of his favorite sayings is: "One should be independent at the age of thirty and at the age of forty one should no longer suffer from perplexities. At age of fifty one should understand the secret of destiny. At the age of sixty one should know the function of truth. At the age of seventy one should be able to follow his heart and be well-behaved."

When A-Lung was fourteen, he read this and asked himself whether he could find the answer earlier? He didn't want to wait until he was seventy. He never stopped searching for the answers to his life's purpose and eventually learned that his original destiny was "to help".

In the process of helping others, he feels happy. Unlike many people who learn techniques and skills in order to make a living, A-Lang realized from one of his many volunteer jobs providing folk massage therapy that he didn't really care about whether he got paid or not. He was happy enough to just see people become healthy. His frustration at the education he received from school made him realize that knowledge for tests, is knowledge in books. It is only when the knowledge is applied that it truly becomes useful. He didn't want his own children to study just to pass exams or academic qualifications. He told them they need to know the purpose for learning, or they might as well find a job that can support them. What matters to A-Lang is "Being able to apply what you have learned." He is a carpenter by trade and spends his days handling wood and machines. He is not good at socializing. To him, most socializing requires a lot of drinking and saying superficial stuff. He always felt exhausted after attending these kinds of occasions. Later he became more and more reserved and stopped attending such social gatherings.

Although serious and quietly spoken he is very conscientious. He won't try to flatter people or make up things just to please his customers. He has a pristine nature concerning justice.

One of the things A-Lang really cares about is the quality of the materials he is using when doing his job. To an untrained observer, you cannot judge by appearances whether the wood has been exposed to toxic preservatives or not. It takes an experienced eye and strong moral principles to determine which materials to use. However, if you give your carpentry projects to A-Lang, you can relax and be at ease. He would never cheat a customer or change the quality of materials just to increase his profits. He will not lie or sacrifice his integrity for money. Lying and cheating are not his game.

A-Lang loves everything about wood.**To him, it has a spiritual quality-an energy. He considers it beautiful from any angle, especially the grain of the wood**; and he believes the rings of the wood are like the traces of wisdom and he loves its aroma.

A-Lang has spent so much time working with wood, it is part of his personality. He is very straightforward and doesn't play around with words. You can talk to him directly without guessing what he means; yes means yes and no means no.

A-Lang's vision is that carpentry should not be limited only to physical labor, for there is knowledge to be shared. He wants to lead his workers to provide lectures and teach younger generations to become skilled carpenters and pass on their hard-won experience. He also wants to help them to plan their retirement and be able to enjoy their later years.

A-Lang considers himself an inflexible carpenter and won't act differently in different situations.

"I am a simple man with a simple view of life, to help others and live my life with honesty and sincerity. What more could I ask for?"

The Self-Reconstruction Determination is his Key to Success
Wen Hsiung Cho（卓文雄）

What is mom？Mother has been a vague concept to Bear (Wen Hsiung) since as long as he could remember because there has been only one other member in his family, his Dad.

Being alone is something he's been used to since he was a child and loneliness has also been his friend.

Therefore, Bear chose to enter the Air Force Machinery School as a PreSergeant right after graduating from junior high school and started living the life of serving his country in the military.

After graduating he entered the Air Force and was transferred to Penghu and then Tamsui. And just like that, 4,000 days passed and Bear learned to be cool with anyone and to deal with colleagues from all over the country.

Who or what is WenQu？In traditional Chinese religious belief, WenQu is the star which takes charge of artistic talents.

Bear has been interested in music and art and perhaps because of the lack of love from his family, he found a sense of belonging in art and has delved deeply into it.

Bear's primary school teacher owned an artist's studio and didn't want to see such great talent vanish with time, so he decided to teach Bear painting skills on his own in his free time. Thanks to this wonderful teacher, Bear has become an excellent painter not only of watercolors and sketches, but also in traditional Chinese painting.

Bear also enjoyed listening to Taiwan's ICRT Radio Channel not because he wanted to learn English, but because he loved Western music. He learned to play the guitar during junior high school and even played in a band in the military.

But having such talent made Bear understand something else, art could only be an interest and not a way to make a living for him because he didn't want to become like those famous painters who gained fame only after death and received nothing for their talents while they were alive. That was certainly not an option on his list. He had to live on his own in this social forest formed by people. So he abandoned art as a career and told himself to be strong and kept reminding himself, "I am the Bear!"

When he finally got tired of military culture, he left the Air Force and started to try out other kinds of jobs. He was a real estate manager, a direct selling agent, a water filter salesman and an organic jewelry store manager. He also learned Zhiwei, Iching, mental counseling and aromatherapy. He even sold something called a "LightWave Energy Patch". Although these jobs seemed inelegant, each of them was a piece of a puzzle to what Bear was going to accomplish in his life.

One day, Bear found his right leg uncomfortable. The doctor diagnosed an injury but couldn't find the exact injured part or reason for it. As a result, they failed to heal his leg. However, this weird problem made Bear a guinea pig for new medical technology and treatments. At that time, the military hospital introduced a method called "Pain Medicine" and Bear was the sixth experimental patient of this special research center, which eventually gave rise to a method of painless childbirth and hospices.

It's hard to determine whether it was luck or bad fortune because as a result of the treatments, Bear began to acquire other problems. But such arrangements of destiny led him to meet a traditional Chinese therapist who had studied at the famous Shaolin Temple. He taught Bear a series of Chigong and massage skills to help Bear recover from those weird problems 20 years ago.

The spiritual comfort he received from Buddhism introduced by the Shaolin doctor had an enormous impact on Bear.

He started studying Buddism as a non-tonsured (partially shaved head) apprentice.

Later on a trip to Nantou in Central Taiwan as part of a rescue team after the notorious "9/21 earthquake" showed Bear how hell could appear on Earth. There he witnessed the combination of anger, grief, fear, desperation and weakness all intertwined together. But he also saw the will of helping and the infinite love of many groups, especially Tzu-Chi.

The anxiety of the rescue teams while they were waiting for the roads to be re-connected with the outside turned into tears when they finally entered the isolated towns. One of the victims of the earthquake told them that they had been the first group of people they had seen since the disaster struck.

After completing the rescue work, Bear became involved in temple building, because he decided that this world needs a lot more love and comfort and there should be more places in it for people to find peace and warmth.

A senior master once asked Bear, **"If the Buddha lives in everything (meaning everything has the potential to become Buddha), even the cells and bacteria, then why do people still get sick?"**

This difficult question led Bear into deep thought for countless days and nights. Finally, Bear figured out the ultimate reason: **Because the way we use our body doesn't coordinate with the way our spirit works.** In other words, the physical body is not synchronized with the spiritual mind. Once our body and spirit find balance, there won't be any more disease or illness.

Bear decided to sift what he had learned, witnessed and experienced for the past 40 years; and then reorganized his experiences into a system of self-reconstruction theory. He believes that the promotion of his healing method will be able to help people become independent of drugs and to keep them from the harm of mistreatment.

"Self-reconstruction can ensure a life without illness as long as one is physically and mentally balanced," Bear says.

As a Loafer Returns
Strive to Step Forward
Cheng-Yuan Lin（林政遠）

Single parent families are something of a tragedy in today's society near the bottom of the population structure pyramid.

No-one would have thought that from the joy of the blessing of wedding vows, however according to the statistic one out of every two married couples in Taiwan would get divorced. It seems the wedding itself is already a preparation for divorce - unless the couples deal with the marriage carefully enough.

A normal and simple boy from Taipei City hit the odds and spent his early childhood in Jian, Hualien. When Cheng-Yuan moved back to Taipei for elementary school, it looked like the best explanation for his school fights was his single parent family background. Cheng-Yuan thought the only way to protect himself was to wave his fists so heavily that they would act as armor and protect him enough to not get bullied.

Cheng-Yuan's mother worked so hard to support their family on her own, that Cheng-Yuan was always conscious of being a burden to her in many ways.

So in order to avoid messing around with violent gangs, he left Taipei shortly after he graduated from junior high school. He started studying on his own and working several part-time jobs. He started his new lifestyle in Hsinchu. This part of his life was the first step in a series of actions of returning as a loafer and realizing his mission in life.

His first real income was earned doing plumbing and electrical work. That was sweat money, but real money. This lifestyle continued until Cheng-Yuan had to do his obligatory term of military service where he graduated from a two-year specialized training school that he attended in the evenings.

Cheng-Yuan later found work at a travel agency as a tour guide. He also worked as a supervisor on construction sites. As long as he could make clean money, he was totally willing to do it.

After leaving the army, Cheng-Yuan became a real estate broker for five years where he made quite a lot of money. He then worked as a chauffeur for the boss of a technology company that sold software games. His unfaltering brightness and tireless hard work permitted him to become the special personal assistant to his boss.

Cheng-Yuan was very appreciative of having such an outstanding mentor and he soon realized he was not far from his goal of success-at least he was walking on the right path for certain.

The fate and experiences Cheng-Yuan has had, have led him to sincerely wish every family in his country and on this planet can be happy, stable, comfortable and beautiful and most importantly, that they can feel secure and safe.

After all, Cheng-Yuan has the memories of his childhood of being harmed through his lack of security and safety.

Because of Cheng-Yuan's thoughtful analysis and suggestions, his boss agreed to support his decision to co-fund and establish a furniture company - ELIZ International Furniture Co., Ltd., which Cheng-Yuan took the full responsibility for operating.

Through their work together, Cheng-Yuan and his boss had built a considerable trust.

Trust is the cornerstone of Cheng-Yuan's career establishment.

Security is the mission of Cheng-Yuan's career development.

The creation of ELIZ Furniture is aimed at providing a feeling of love, happiness and security. Cheng-Yuan's desire is **to create the feeling of belonging and joy by changing the settings and layouts of a space through which he hopes to prevent the appearance of more single parent families in Taiwan.**

Thus it is said, **"As a loafer returns the fortune wheel turns. Half study, half working will change a stone into gold."**

And **as the feelings of happiness and security are created, in Taiwan there should be no more single parent families.**

Handmade Soap Legend
Unyielding Belief
Hsin-An Lin (林信安)

Hsin-An and his grandfather often went up to the mountains to collect herbs and he experienced the magnificent beauty of botanical plants.

In 1993, Hsin-An graduated from National Cheng-Chi University, majoring in advertising and took a job working alongside his wife at a foreign bank. He and his wife had a simple and happy life together. After giving birth to their first child, Hsin-An's wife decided to quit her job at the bank and become a full-time mother. Consequently by accident, she discovered her interest in handmade soaps. Hsin-An discussed with his wife if she would be interested in starting a business to sell her soaps. He was happy to finally have the chance to develop his own specialty and create a business model through internet marketing. This endeavor would mean turning over a new leaf in his life.

In 2009, Hsin-An officially ended his career with the bank, and set ahead at full steam on Love Herbology. He has never forgotten his time as a hardworking farmer along with his childhood wish to help other farmers to improve their toiling lifestyle. However that time was only a beginning.

In 2014, to lend a hand to farmers in Taiwan, Hsin-An directed a project to establish the Green Agricultural Development Association which has gathered leaders in the field of agriculture-related business to offer whatever they can for Taiwan, for agriculture, for ecology as well as for the Earth.

Good material stands out among competitors.

Love Herbology rapidly became an unexpected winner for its unique entrepreneurial ideas as well as its excellent quality soaps. In addition to Taiwan itself, the handmade soaps are marketed in China, Japan, Hong Kong, and Singapore. Many media outlets have actively reported stories about the Love Herbology legend, including Apple Daily, Liberty Times, ETTV, CTV News and Hong Kong U Magazine. Since then, the reputation of Love Herbology brand of **natural, toxin-free**, herbal soaps has been widely acclaimed, owing much to the idea of seeking an ultimate in the healthy ways of making its products.

Hsin-An doesn't mind copycat competitors, because his nonstop creativity and broad perspective make them unable to catch up.

Hsin-An knows the way to integrate local features and cultural concepts into his product and through his actions, not only meets the satisfaction of his customers' spirit but also shows how he loves his homeland of Taiwan.

Then, just as Hsin-An's market scale was expanding, his biggest customer passed away. They had been cooperating so closely that this caused a crisis and it came as a bolt from the blue.

However, Hsin-An made use of every possible marketing mechanism, coordinating competitors as well as connecting with different businesses. The authors were so inspired that they joined in his Green Agricultural Development Association to open a new line of essential oils and create a spectacular win-win situation. Such wisdom has no doubt turned crisis into opportunity.

As the recent cooking oil storm took place in Taiwan, many local industries stumbled tragically. But Hsin-An was one of the first to invite reporters to examine and inspect the materials that Love Herbology had been using. Hsin-An really had done his business honestly and with outstanding vision.

Hsin-An remarks, "There are plenty of methods for making money, but I choose to build my reputation established by trusted and worry-free products, rather than to risk reputation to become notorious.

"A man can do everything. He can also choose not to. We may make money today, but Karma will return to us tomorrow."

Thus it is said: **To love our own land and nature we must wash out the ignorance and show our wisdom.**

Saving the Earth with ecologic agriculture is a sacred job for Hsin-An Lin.

The Law of Attraction Accountant
Chun-Ting Lin（林俊廷）

Being a "mama's boy" is nobody's fault.

Ever since Chun-Ting was born he never had to worry about food or clothing and his mother pampered him so much that he was considered a "mama's boy". In traditional Chinese culture, this may have been considered as being born with luck.

However, Chun-Ting was not proud of being pampered. Instead he felt inferior to others. He was not happy because he had that strong desire burning in his heart to prove that he was not a mama's boy. He wanted to gain the respect of others and build his self-esteem. Eventually, he made a lot of breakthroughs and accomplished tasks and efforts ordinary people couldn't have imagined.

At the age of 22, it was Chun-Ting's time to serve in the military. Instead of asking his elders to make special arrangements and try to attain an easy position for him, he followed all the requirements to become a naval officer. Drifting on the waves, singing on the deck of a ship and watching the boundless ocean, Chun-Ting felt he was independent and a grown up for the first time in his life.

Chun-Ting doesn't expect himself to be mighty and brave, but to be an articulate and attractive super-lecturer. He demands of himself to have the ability to speak clearly and eloquently in front of his clients. He knows he needs take any opportunity he can to practice and he never rejects any invitation to speak publicly. "It takes ten years of practice to be able to perform three minutes perfectly on the stage." Chun-Ting gets on the stage again and again but still feels defeated over and over.

He clearly knows it takes onstage charisma to be able to become a popular and powerful speaker. He started to read widely and accumulate experience in life. He was not afraid of anything and had endless courage. He started his next adventure in life by opening a bookkeeping firm with his best friends from college. Sometimes partners can go through thick and thin together but can't share the blessing. His friends passed their exam and became Certified Accountants but Jin-Ting didn't. The distribution of profit became unfair and uncomfortable for everyone in the firm. They ended up breaking their partnership.

Chun-Ting felt extremely discouraged and immersed himself in Mahjong for three days and nights. After that he motorcycled around the island and followed that by just dawdling around. He could have won the "Goof-off of the Year Award," if there were such a thing. This kind of self-cheating life continued until he met the girl when he was 33 years old. To pursue this graceful beauty, Chun-Ting now had another goal in life. He started to go to the library to pander to her wishes. He became inspired by his love affair 詩書氣自華. He turned over a new leaf and fell in love with books. He decided to take the CPA exam again. Finally, he became a certified accountant after 10 years of trying and now he owns his own accounting firm. It takes extreme perseverance and willpower to fulfill this kind of dream.

In order to further improve himself, he began running. He got into the habit of long distance running and participated in over 20 marathons. He could run for 150 minutes without any breaks. He forced himself and trained his ability to endure.

And eventually the Prince and Princess got married.

This long journey of self-discipline has tempered Chun-Ting to become a real and responsible man who can take on impossible tasks. He has become a humorous, energetic and magical accountant and attractive lecturer on stage.

It was his destiny that he was born into a wealthy family. All of his investments paid off. The son of nobility has transformed. Let's applaud and congratulate Chun-Ting.

Bitterness Ends, Sweetness Begins
Queen of Military Residences
Chun-Jung Lin（林春蓉）

Vivian (Chun-Jung) was born into a family with five boys and three girls. She was a lovely and adorable child. A distant relative took her for a couple of days and asked her parents to adopt her, heedless of her Vivian's well-being. Although an uncommon practice at that time, Vivian was given no choice and couldn't resist. It was to be her fate. Vivian's life became a miserable and tragic TV drama. Her early childhood was similar to the script of the Japanese drama "Oshin."

Vivian's stepmother was a widow. Whenever she worked she would leave Vivian and her step-brother at the homes of other relatives. Vivian learned the hard lessons of survival by the age of three, when others her age were still being loved by their own parents. She experienced both cold and warm care every day of her childhood. She was confused about whether she was adopted or abandoned. Her life was soaked with tears and bitterness. She grew up without any fixed living place and transferred to three different elementary schools.

Her life was exclusive of any fun. As a bony and malnourished girl, her life was burning wood, gathering rice, harvesting other crops and watering plants and fertilizing them.

Once she cut herself while preparing food for the ducks and the food was dyed in her blood. She was so afraid that she would be beaten again and she knew her relatives wouldn't care about the injury. She shivered with pain and fear. Her only first aid was to use tears to clean her bleeding wound.

Later in life her stepmother remarried to a small store owner who sold rice and quilts. Her stepmother considered the marriage a blessing but for Vivian it was the beginning of more misery.

This man had a wife and sons before this marriage and most of his income went to them. What was left for Vivian was heavy-handed and sweat-filled labor. Her delicate and dainty body was used to carry heavily loaded packages of rice, to set up the stands to sell goods and to take care of her little brother who was nine years younger.

She worked and studied whenever she could find the time. She passed the entrance exam for the first girls' high school in Keelung, but her stepmother didn't want to Vivian's to continue learning and so made her go to the National Keelung Vocational High School of Business And Technology. Vivian took a part-time job to support her own studies while continuing help at her stepfather's "family business." All the while she studied.

The deity of Fortune finally came into Vivian's life after she graduated from the professional school. She found work with a business in Keelung and was promoted from bookkeeper to special assistant to an executive working in Hong Kong. Her sixteen years of on-the-job training had cultivated Vivian's abilities and her character for all the requirements of success. She could never express enough her gratitude for this valuable lifetime advisor. She eventually also realized her most desired dream of obtaining a Bachelor's Degree in International Trading.

When Vivian was thirty, her lifetime mentor and advisor passed away and incredibly, the true love of her life appeared at the same time. Vivian finally escaped from the place which had scarred her soul and came to Taipei.

Upon arrival in Taipei, her new challenge became selling apartments used by military personnel. She knocked on every single door in the area. She walked until she had blisters on her feet placing ads into mail boxes and with callused hands and a smile on her sweaty face she distributed fliers to passers-by.

With her feet on the ground she made an industrious and diligent effort to build her own territory from the apartments of military personnel. Even when her partners had left for other work, Vivian chose to stay focused on real estate for "people's homes."

Her choice gave her the time and energy to balance between her job and her family. It was the happiness Vivian had waited for, for such a long time.

Life is full of surprises and choices and one day she was approached by the owner of H&B Housing who told her that he didn't want to run the company anymore and gave her two days to consider if she would take the business over. With the expectations of her co-workers and encouragement from her family, Vivian took a leap of faith and became the director of her own business for life!

Vivian is proud that "integrity and passion" are not only their slogan, but also their fundamental belief.

Selling skill is not their key to success. What they have is sincerity and a professional, sharing mind. It is their commitment to their clients that they will accomplish and achieve every mission with which they are entrusted. They have never had litigation or appeals from any clients since Vivian became the owner of their company. Her goal is to overcome any impossible assignment in the real estate industry.

Vivian grew up in a tragic and ill-fated circumstance but it became her motivation to strive tirelessly for prosperity. She didn't want to drift in the stream all her life. She wanted to transform herself from a water lotus to a brilliant hibiscus tree.

Soul Guidance
Kuei-Ju Lin（林桂如）

The movie "A Vessel on an Endless Ocean" makes viewers shed many tears. The leading character Feng-Xi Cheng is from Kou-hu, Yunlin, where Kuei-Ju Lin was born in 1969.

Kuei-Ju has outstanding logic and is gifted with the power of intuition. Her childhood background is unknown but doesn't really matter. Kuei-Ju says, "I don't even remember my own blood type."

After finishing her studies, she gained much experience as a business consultant and in company training and education. She also promoted soul music for eight years. Kuei-Ju has many certificates concerning the connections of body, mind, and soul, including **Neuro-Linguistic Programming.**

With deep religious beliefs, Kuei-Ju found her own life mission. Five years ago she decided to start a business of her own, mainly providing service as a psychological consultant focusing on brain development and energy sessions. She hopes to give proper assistance to people who want to bring back energy to their lives.

A book titled "Inner Talk" written by an American master of brain development is a resource that keeps Kuei-Ju pushing forward in her daily life, learning, and sleep. It influences the subconscious through highly positive energy and inner coordination to produce miraculous beliefs and vigorous power of self-healing, conquering depression and melancholy. It helps people maintain a forever young internal optimism, reinforces self-discipline and builds high self-esteem to achieve positive interpersonal relationships. You will believe yourself to be a genius and take action immediately. You will be led toward a wealthy and happy life. The effectiveness of sonic technology may be a myth to many people, but there are many others, including the author, who have truly benefitted from it.

The energy class is about developing your own energy field from the base chakra to crown chakra. The seven chakra concept comes from the wisdom of ancient Indian religious practices by which one can make the body-mind-soul reach a harmonious balance.

Kuei-Ju has consulted more than a thousand cases. Her abundant experience has cultivated a great empathy and mercy. Without ego, in Kuei-Ju's world there exist no extreme emotions. Kuei-Ju practices and promotes the law of attraction to assist many to change their patterns of thinking and to generate success in people who are fighting for their lives.

Deeply influenced by her mother, Kuei-Ju has understood since junior high school to listen to her classmates' psychological issues. Life with a husband is like living with a senior in chakra practice for certainly, the insistence of the heart to serve and to devote is sometimes stricken. Kuei-Ju wishes to improve her ability to help people so she works non-stop in order to elevate herself.

Seven years ago Kuei-Ju was invited to join Business Network International but the first three weeks at the Chang-Xin Chapter made her dizzy because the magnetic field matched her so poorly that she wanted to leave the team. At that moment, a message was sent into her mind: you have a mission to help the people on this team to understand the lessons in their lives, to expand their abilities and to actively serve more people.

Kuei-Ju used her willpower, strong desire and passion and contributed time and effort to being a chairwoman at the Chang-Xin Chapter for three years. Initially with only twelve members, she led the first team in Taiwan to become a Platinum Branch. Kuei-Ju's actions have stimulated other branches to motivate their teams to move forward.

When there is a bigger wish, there is a bigger power. Through much effort, Chang-Xin branch finally reached more than 50 members and in April, 2013, they became the first Platinum Branch in Taiwan, along with Chang-Rung branch.

Double Platinum leads to double the glory.

Kuei-Ju has knowledge of the three elements of the universe - material, energy, and message but she has difficulty in delivering her love to people who don't understand. From time to time it results in misunderstandings and negative reactions. However, she chooses to confront it calmly. She has many emotions within her while others sense only joy and happiness.

Just because we don't understand something doesn't mean it doesn't exist. It's just that we haven't yet obtained the wisdom and power to realize it, thus we can only be amazed by the creations of our universe.

What Kuei-Ju does or thinks is not necessarily understood by everyone. Like a lonely vessel in the ocean, it may take a lot of energy to move along but it will never lose its direction, with a beacon in its heart. Thus it is said, **"A vessel on the endless ocean steers souls to the skyline."**

A "None Business" Woman
Jin-Wu Lin（林瑾梧）

The Girl's Festival (the seventh day of the seventh lunar month) is Jin-Wu's birthday. She was born next-door to the spiritual Temple of Confucius, a propitious omen.

Be that as it may,the early years of her life were far from fortuitous. On the contrary, they were filled withtragedy and hardship, primarily featuring the incessant fighting of her parents. Her father was a truck driver and was the one who put food on the table for the family. But frequently they were unable to make ends meet. Therefore, from a very young age, Jin-Wuwould work with her grandmother collecting scraps on the streets and selling them for money.

She describesthe scene that was to be a defining moment for her family. One late night, the same nightmare for Jin-Wu played again. Her father beat up her mother severely and her mother had no choice but to escape from him. Her mother took Jin-Wu with her on their way running and looking for shelter. Jin-Wu saw blood flowing down from her mother's head mixing with the down poured rain. They took shelter in a factory. But when sheawoke the next morning, she was astonished to be severely reprimanded by her father; and her mother received a cruelbeating. Jin-Wuwas only four and following this incident her mother left home, never to return. Jin-Wu was the third child, with an elder brother and sister and one younger brother. The only tasty food she could remember from her childhood was a sip of powdered milk she had made for her younger brother. And she was so short that she had to stand on a stool to reach the kitchen counter.

Jin-Wu's sister had been brain damagedfrom a fever when she was a baby. She was very slow to react.

Her father made them go to school together. Jin-Wu was only six but she already knew that she had to protect her eight-year-old sister. Her father frequently indulged in drinking and when he felt the children had done something wrong, he would ask them to stand in line and as punishment would make them listen to his stories of his harsh and hard-working life. He was easily agitated and started beating the children. When this happened, their grandfather would take the elder brother away and their grandmother would rescue the younger brother. Her father would not beat up her sister for she was sick. So Jin-Wu was the one who was beaten the most. She can still remember the whipping sound from her father's stick, even today.

This chain of disasters tempered her personality.

After graduating from junior high school she worked in a textile factory. By the first month, she had already become proficient in packaging, embroidery, pressing pedals and tagging. Her boss there became one of her life-time advisors. He helped her to go to night school at the Jinwen Professional School. She worked part-time at a men's suit store after her first boss went abroad to recover his health.

The guard at her night school helped her to find work at the school until her graduation. One year later she decided to help her brothers in curtain manufacturing business at the request of her father. That was the beginning of her career. She has devoted herself to this career for more than 30 years.

She and her brothers were courageous enough to start their own company,not withstanding that there were competitors everywhere. They had a unique view and a burning desire for success. "Let's be the most professional, the most hard-working and the best in the field." That was the first time Jin-Wu had shown her decisive power.

Because of her experience working in the textile factory, Jin-Wu could make all the curtains herself but they had to hire other workers to make the wallpaper, carpets and ceramic floors, thus greatly increasing their costs. They revealed theirwisdom and skill for the second time and made a critical decision. "Let's focus on making curtains only. It will reduce our outlay and make us more professional."

They realized it would take new knowledge and new skill to become the most professional; and so their search began. They imported books and magazines and they paid translators so they could read them. They fumbled around and over the new knowledge until eventually they made it become their own.

They went through many stages of trials and errors because they had no precedence to follow and they made many mistakes. The costs and trouble for their experience could not be comprehended by others in the great system of the Industry Association.

But their hard work finally bore fruit. They created their own proprietary method. This was their greatest breakthrough. Under the firm and decisive leadership, the whole family paved the way to their own success. "J.J.Curtain" had seven workers who made curtains. Their own team kept on growing and "J.J.Curtain" created a legendary success together.

However, a calamity hit their family and their business when Jin-Wu's younger brother was diagnosed with carcinoma of the mouth. After the torment of a series of operations and chemotherapy he was beyond recognition and before he reached the age of 40, God took his life.

It was a nightmare for Jin-Wu. How could she face the pain of losing the brother she had cared for all her life?

In this atmosphere of pain and grief she made a choice:to be strong and unyielding, for they had a business to run and employees to pay. That was her social duty.

Jin-Wu continued leading the company as the director. She walked the talk and earned the respect of her customers and treated her workers like family, sharing with them the benefits of their production and company profits.

The company's performance rose to a new level and instead of falling back, they advanced steadily. To observers, it was amazing but to Jin-Wu there was no other choice.

Her brother had meant the world to her family and she knew nothing could be more precious than to realize his vision. Her only wish was that her brother could rest in peace and reach a place where he could find joy.

Jin-Wu realizes that the value of life is measured in neither fame nor wealth. It is how you use your life to benefit others.

She wants to lead those passionate and dynamic curtain masters into serving society and fighting for the economy of Taiwan. She also wants her clients feel that **when they open a window, there is hope in the world and when they close their curtains, there is warmth and safety in their homes.**

She may not have been born to be the center beam but she has become a supporting pillar. She may not have been the main meal, but without her there would be no dessert. It might have seemed bitter at the beginning, but finally, in the end, sweetness arrives.

Hence, it is said that **Jin-Wu is certainly carved from jade and** helps without ego. Having endured so much hardship, she has built her own legend in the curtain industry and by cultivating herself, she has become a lighthouse for others.

The Confidence Chemise Maker
Yan-Ting Lin（林讌庭）

It is not easy to describe a woman as great as Yan-Ting's mother in such a short story. She is the most highly respected and loved person in Yan-Ting's life, so we will dedicate this article to her.

Other than tribal natives and some so-called nudists, all human bodies portrayed in history books are covered with something. That is to emphasize in our heritage for future generations that clothing provides some sense of protection and security. Thus, exquisite taste in underwear has had its role in the evolutionary history of human civilization.

Many poignant stories happened during the period in Taiwan's history in which the Kuomintang (KMT) retreated from Mainland China to Taiwan (around 1950). A great tea merchant gave his quietest daughter away to an old couple who couldn't produce children themselves. It was unfair to the little girl, because she could have enjoyed the fortune and comfortable life-style of her original family. Adoption in Taiwan during that period was really common. The little girl undertook the many burdens of her tough life in order to help support her new family. After graduating from elementary school, she made the decision to learn a specific competence in order to put food on the table for her family and to help reverse their existing circumstances. She accepted an offer to be an apprentice to a master chemisette maker and for three years and eight months she learned how to make chemisettes at one of Taiwan's most prosperous companies, called Chun Hua Shopping Malls.

At that time, being an apprentice in such a store meant living like a servant. She was expected to do many odd jobs and chores for her masters while endeavoring to master her craft. All the many challenges Yan-Ting's mother faced did not beat her down, instead she hardened and strengthened herself and became more determined to succeed. She used her meager savings to learn from different masters and gradually gained recognition from their many customers. Through her hard work, study and application, Yan-Ting's mother began to develop her abilities and soon started attracting her own customers.

After perfecting her skills and developing an outstanding reputation she got married and opened up her first chemisette store and, although her shop was very small, she dreamed of great success. She would sometimes dream that every stitch would raise the confidence of each woman who bought from her store and that her threads would sew the beauty of their happiness. With her artful creations and good intentions, she made countless chemisettes for her many satisfied customers.

Yan-Ting actually grew up in the little chemisette store. She played underneath the sewing table and matured with the rhythm of the sewing machine. Her mother supported her throughout her childhood with her unique artwork. Yan-Ting is so familiar with what she sees and hears in the chemisette store. It has been in her blood since she was in her mother's womb. It could be interpreted as the perfect prenatal education. Yan-Ting considers that she has inherited her mother's spirit and skill and promotes them as her mission in life.

After graduating from the Department of Fashion Design at Shih Chien University, she became the assistant designer for Wacoal (a brand of women's lingerie). She learned a combination of Western and Eastern sewing skills and tries to merge the elements of the classical beauty of Chinese women with the romantic styles of the West. She researched and analyzed ergonomics and continuously tested, innovated and advanced her art. She made every effort to achieve perfection only to deliver her mother's great gift and spirit. With her persistent and skillful work, her store "Rawa Designers" became well known and very popular.

Yan-Ting insists on proper measuring and custom sizing. The chemisettes are tailored to fit perfectly to a woman's figure and provide gentle protection and extreme comfort at the same time. The chemisettes allow ladies to enhance their graceful figures and positive charm. With Yan-Ting's creations, you don't have to sacrifice your health for the sake of beauty and an elegant countenance. The author asked Yan-Ting why she still insists on producing only custom-made merchandise. Wouldn't it be more profitable to produce large quantities at one time? Doesn't custom making each item raise the cost and lower the profits?

Yan-Ting believes money is a necessary tool for survival but we shouldn't become slaves to money. "If I don't live my life the way I want to live, in the way that my mother taught me to live, then where is the difference between an animal and a human being?"

"There are no fingerprints or eyes that are exactly the same. Even twins have their own distinctive features. There aren't any two exact pairs of breasts. So how can we justify having every single breast sized by cups?"

"Most women have a mistaken concept about the size of their breasts. It's actually a sign of a lack of confidence. However, if you choose the wrong underwear, it can not only cause great discomfort, but it could also influence your health.

Women should dress themselves for more than just vanity and to please men." Our mind will influence our bodies. Our appearances and bodies reflect the condition of our mind. It is a serious attract to women when we learn that we suffered breast cancers and had to do breast surgeries to keep our lives. Therefore, Rawa Designers devoted themselves to rehabilitate their confidence with customer made chemises. Yan Ting wants to activate these plans in order to give breast cancer patients brilliant confident and hope.

Rawa Designers has been operating for more than 50 years and has never advertised. They generate their ample business turnover through fine product quality and constant word of mouth recommendations from their many loyal customers.

Yan-Ting says that she does care about money, but she only wants to earn it through integrity and sincerity. "Seeing the contentment, health, confidence and happiness of our customers after wearing one of our undergarments is the most satisfying payback for my job. What we produce is not simply an undergarment. Our vision is to help create a graceful figure for all women and to build a free and easy spirit in women's hearts. We want to encourage a unique self-confidence in Taiwanese women."

Hence it is said: **To put on a corset for confidence, go to a small shop with a large vision.**

The Magician who Brings Boundless Pleasure
Magical Director
Chuan-Hsiang Wu（武傳翔）

Chuan-Hsiang Wu's ancestors were doctors who practiced Chinese medicine in Jiansu in ancient China and even served the royal family during the imperial Qin dynasty.

Chuan-Hsiang's father does missile research but doesn't serve in the military or government. His mother is an elementary school teacher. He has one elder sister, three years older than he, who is a marketing expert with a good relationship with her family. In this family of diverse educational backgrounds, Chuan-Hsiang was born with a gift for magic.

From an early age, watching magic on TV, he would figure out how the tricks were done and he developed his natural talent with no outside instruction. Chuan-Hsiang started making money performing magic in high school. He established a magic society in Hsin-chu Senior High School and taught magic to his fellow classmates. Out of a forty-member class, thirty of them knew how to perform poker tricks. His society became popular and very well known.

In the beginning, Chuan-Hsiang didn't know there were magic props-instead, he brought his magic to life using simple methods and only rudimentary materials.

When he came to understand that the best magic performances required professional stage props, he also realized that magic was a very costly job to do.

However, Chuan-Hsiang wasn't motivated by money. In order to discover and understand the roots of magic he traveled on his own to America, Great Britain, China, Japan, Korea, Italy, Thailand, Singapore, Hong Kong and the Philippines. His pilgrimage led him to the conclusion that the professional magic industry really was a mess.

His conclusion was based on the fact that people think magic is merely a performance, a scheme, a fraud; or a trick by young men to pick up girls. This was a huge insult to the real traditions of magic.

Chuan-Hsiang sees magic as a true art form. He has been called "con man" all his life but he preserves the hope that one day people will see him differently.

At one point in his life, he moved to Silicon Valley in California. There he decided to dedicate himself to magic and to make it his personal art form.

Chuan-Hsiang graduated from Art College as a Master of Stage Directing. He thought no-one would believe in a young director so he continued to train himself in order to gain mature credibility.

He loves the theater, not movies because what touches him most is real-time performance, not editing. He wants the one and only, not a repetition because magic is inherently theatrical. **Chuan-Hsiang has devoted himself to magic-to making the impossible possible.**

"The greatest magic is enchantment, creating real illusions. Enchantment is a magic no one can solve. It is the best performance art with nothing to hide."

Chuan-Hsiang expects to establish a magic school to cultivate future magicians who will bring audiences amazement, hope and encouragement.

To Chuan-Hsiang, magic is the true gift of heaven, which creates even more gifts such as great friends and mentors on the way to performing. Chuan-Hsiang is grateful for everyone's help and appreciation.

Chuan-Hsiang also says it is easy to make money performing magic and easy to lose yourself in it, too. But to damage magic to make money violates the principles of magic. One cannot destroy the beauty and mystery for one's own personal gain. To Chuan-Hsiang, magic is priceless and his performances are valuable as the work of a theatrical director.

Spread Your Wings and Fly Away
I-Jui Hung（洪逸瑞）

On April 8th, 1964-the Buddha's birthday-a special man was born in Taiwan and his life since then has been a series of miracles.

Born into a poor family, Larry (I-Jui) started working part-time after entering Chien-kuo Senior High School. He also worked for the four years he was studying at the History Department, Fu-jen University and the Graduate School of Management Science in Tamkang University. He has a way of reaching new levels of awareness and attaining new goals by constantly studying deeper and further, so Larry always fundamentally considers himself a "part-timer."

As a result of his father's strict discipline, Larry has cultivated a meticulous, upright and plainspoken personality. He has also evolved the ability to master his inner passions and so has developed a strong internal resolve tempered by his innate sassiness.

His private life is a mystery but he is known to be a man of wisdom, able to know something profoundly by seeing only a little of it.

He tends the bonsai trees and flowers on his balcony from where he can see the mountains and forest. From his sofa in the living room he reads books and newspapers but he also obtains knowledge and wisdom from ancient times to the present. He watches movies alone in the city but he is also inspired to contemplate and create the future.

The author asked him about setbacks in his life. Larry answers, "Every day we encounter challenges and setbacks." Then, Larry smiles modestly, saying the biggest setback for him has been his "loss of memory." From this we can see how reserved a person he really is.

Loss of memory is just a humorous excuse for avoiding discussion of his negative past. He wants instead to focus on positive energy and is always lifting himself up. Loss of memory is also a demonstration of his selflessness. He does not really care to discuss himself and his goal orientation tends to focus on others.

"If there are worries in life, that's because people are having problems remembering what should be remembered and forgetting what should be forgotten," he says.

Larry does not have many worries because he is only and always thinking of methods and plans to accomplish his future goals.

"I have a limited brain capacity," he says. "That's why I can only remember these things."

His fondest accomplishment was reaching 6th place in the Government Official Special Exams. But he chose not to take a job in government service. He loves the freedoms and challenges of the business life much more than the rules and regulations of a government position.

Studying history, Larry indeed has a good memory. He knows many details, big and small about China's history and overseas, from ancient times to modern. He has spent many hours researching Taiwan's economic environment and development and has dedicated himself to understanding the global finance industry, including large corporations such as: Citi Bank, China Trust, Standard Chartered and Cathay Bank. He has garnered a great deal of knowledge and abundant experience programming consumer financial products, analyzing customer values and setting up and executing marketing strategies. He has also taken part in training programs with these institutions and has many related certificates. Even Citi Bank and Standard Chartered awarded him for his outstanding services.

As a consequence of his knowledge of the finance industry, Larry transferred to real estate which is on a parallel plane with the finance world.

Founded upon his devotion to teamwork and his educational training, Larry decided to join in Business Networking International's referral platform. He held the position of chairman at the Chang-Fa branch in Taipei and was awarded many honors and eventually he accepted the challenge to start his own branch.

On the auspicious occasion of its grand opening in July 2013, BNI Chang-Zhan branch started with a record 51 people and began functioning in Taiwan. Other branches are like newborn babies but this team was a dark horse, showing up to amaze everyone. It very soon became the fifth biggest branch in the world with more than 80 members in 2014. Their extraordinary performance has made their Taiwanese partners so proud.

However, success never comes by chance. The key to success of the rise of the Chang-Zhan team is Larry's leadership. There were indeed setbacks and hardships. To expand from the initial five people to fifteen was fast, but to reach fifty needed time. The goal-oriented Larry kept encouraging and contributing vision, hope and confidence to his team. They prepared everything they needed and planned the complete process in meticulous detail and, after only five and a half months, achieved their victory-an unforgettable occasion for their founding 51 team members.

In the history of business networking, Larry has written his own page. Larry is now focused on his next goal.

"There's nothing that can't be done, it's only a matter of people wanting it or not. As long as I want it, there's nothing that can't be achieved."

Thus it is said, **"The black horse rides a thousand miles to write his own history with greatness and with honor."**

A Man so great that No Words can describe Him Properly Made in Taiwan
Hsu, Hung (許宏)

Hsu, Hung was born in the poor rural area of Jinguashi. As children, he and his friends ran barefoot in the fields, napped on Banyan trees and felt the coolness and sunlight between the leaves. Occasionally caterpillars would fall on their faces and they would put them back gently to the trees looking forward to meeting them as colorful butterflies. They didn't know what an air conditioner was, so slept shirtless on the floor to cool down.

There were fish and shrimp in the stream and they played hide and seek with the crabs. He loved to get up at three o'clock to climb the mountains in order to watch the distant sun rise from behind the sea.

He had aboriginal neighbors from the A-Mei tribe and they enjoyed singing heartily, accompanied by guitars. This kind of simple life was happy. Some nights he would lie on the stone floor at the entrance to his house, contemplating the stars and wondering where he was from. Tears would wet his face for no reason.

In second grade, he found he could write music although he didn't really know anything about music theory and could easily play many familiar melodies. He might have been talented but he didn't dare to dream of being a singer.

During high school, he thought only violent fighting was considered "masculine" and so was under probation most of the time. And although he held the honor of Number One student at school, he could not make up for the embarrassment his parents felt. He lost his direction in life and gave up on entering college and instead became a gangster at the casinos.

One day he was reading Sun Tzu's On the Art of War and suddenly realized how impulsive and reckless he had been. That realization ended his selfish and irrational period of teenage irresponsibility.

He wanted to stop living the life of a criminal so went to Chengtian Temple in Tucheng City to look for the truths of life. During a resting period while chopping wood with one of the ascetic monks, he asked the master for **the definition of "brotherhood"**. The master looked into his eyes and replied, **"Being a Buddhist, what you need is compassion not brotherhood. Young men should stay away from violence and killing."** He was touched and had a sudden realization and the tears dropped from his face like rain.

He went home joyfully and found his mother cooking. He held her gently and said, **"Mom, starting from today I will be a vegetarian."**

He spent the next two years doing his mandatory military service on an isolated island, only going home twice. The experiences of those two years led to an important stage in his transformation. He also had a true feeling of freedom on finishing military service and coming back to Taiwan. **He kneeled down and kissed the ground. It was the smell of his mother land.**

After that he studied for two months at a cram school and became a student of Tamkang University where he graduated with a Master's Degree in Chemistry. During those brilliant years he wrote songs, played in a band, taught guitar and also taught at cram school. He knew in his heart that he didn't have any time to waste

Although starting as a trainer at one of the leading pharmaceutical companies, he was more involved in the marketing of skin care, health foods and essential oils. It is such a fantastic thing to make people beautiful and healthy. After a speech he made in Singapore, he was head hunted to work there and he started his overseas career, becoming familiar with the people and the markets of south-east Asia. That was the first time that he had a truly expansive perspective on life.

In 2005 he chose to come back to Taiwan to devote his knowledge and ability to becoming a business consultant, helping industries to establish their cooperative culture and professional operating systems. He also published four different books in one year regarding success, beauty product marketing and leadership. He also edited a book about DIY Feng-Shui for his father Xu, Sheng-Xiong. All of these books are still popular today.

Later in 2008 under the urge of social responsibility, he established his own company focusing on providing professional skin care products, health care products and essential oils with professional education and training.

His company has its own factory guided by their own ethics principles and insisting on only the highest quality ingredients. They not only sell but also manufacture all the products themselves. They know their roots are in Taiwan and therefore they must grow with honesty and integrity.

Hsu, Hung's company has made and set many records and they maintain that winning attitude. They want to use the essential oils from their factory to spread the fragrances of Taiwan to the whole world.

Essential oil is the critical element in perfume. In many cases however, chemical essence has replaced the use of natural ingredients. To Hsu, Hung, he is a revolution in perfume that has started **in Taiwan.**

He is striving to change people's concept of perfume and rearrange their olfactory neurons. He hopes that when people talk about perfume and essential oil they also think about Taiwan.

Hsu, Hung is an artist and a musician but he is also a Taiwanese and although his background is humble, he appreciates everything Taiwan offers to the world.

Scaling the Heights
Optimistic All the Time
Feng-Jung Hsu（許峯榮）

Feng-Jung Hsu is known by his nickname "Da-Shan" (Big Mountain). The name not only represents his towering figure but is also related to his work experiences. If all the categories of his past jobs were piled up they would be as tall as a mountain.

Da-Shan was an outstanding basketball player during his high school years and took advantage of his great height to earn fame as an all-round athlete. Unfortunately, he fell while slam dunking and was injured and that was the end of his basketball dream.

After graduating from college, he worked as a waiter in both Eastern and Western restaurants and also in their kitchens. He has been a cook, a courier, a representative for a printing company. He has worked in a paper factory and has been a businessman in telemarketing. He has also been a manager in various areas: biotechnology, the environmental protection industry, in advertising and in telecommunications. Any job you could imagine, he has been in it.

However, a rolling stone gathers no moss and transferring from job to job provided little enrichment.

Da-Shan's businesses always seemed to tumble unexpectedly. Eventually, he invested in an environmental biotechnology company with one of his business partners. With the concept of microbial decomposition, they developed a set of special products and also provided technical services. Da-Shan was in charge of all the budgeting and expenses and developed the marketing strategies and scouted for clients. He even handled the disgusting details like going into the septic tanks himself.

He was quite content even in adversity. As the company finances gradually entered blissful circumstances, his partner set him up with an outsider who lured Da-Shan into a trap and all efforts he had devoted were brought to nought.

His company was invaded and occupied. This destroyed not only his business, but also his belief in humanity. He was in total despair.

Fortunately, soon after he married a wonderful woman with tremendous patience, consideration and understanding. She helped guide Da-Shan to God and he was able to gather himself to confront the challenges of his life and to regain his trust in people. He eventually climbed up from the lowest ebbs of his life.

That is the power of faith in religion and the true meaning of love. Even though faced with the ups and downs of his business and under extreme pressure, he was able to end his log time addiction to smoking.

There were two strong motivating factors for him to do so. Firstly, his wife only gave him NT$100 (around US $3 dollars) a day for living expenses and she told him that if he were a responsible man, he would quit smoking. Otherwise, if he got sick or died from lung cancer, whose fault would it be? Her words moved Da-Shan like an earthquake and he decided to quit smoking immediately.

In recent years, with the explosive development of smart phone technology, the mobile commerce industry has become one of the most promising business models available. Consequently, Da-Shan partnered with his best friends David Zhang and Yi Yong Zhang to form a professional team to fully engage in the development of mobile commerce applications.

They cooperated to become masters in their field. He knows the limitations of individual effort compared with the synergy of sincere cooperation. Now they had three earnest men working together and all heading in the same direction.

Da-Shan's enthusiasm for business was back. The team has successfully pushed high quality products manufactured in Taiwan into Mainland China, Japan and various countries through mobile commerce apps. Also with the Backpack Travel in Taiwan project, the number of tourists from Mainland China has increased and the orders for "Made in Taiwan" souvenirs through their app system has sky-rocketed.

There are no words to describe their excitement. At that moment, Da-Shan had a sudden realization why he had gone through so many different job experiences. They helped him to grasp the needs of his clients and to improve his ability to catch the niche market. All the arrangements turned out for the best for him.

As a native of Taiwan, Da-Shan vows in his heart that he will do his best to promote all the best qualities of Made in Taiwan products to glorify Taiwan.

It's the ultimate goal of their team to have all their products from Taiwan to become the best.

It has been a winning and glorious moment for Da-Shan. He is firmly committed to keeping on pushing himself and learning to make his dreams and goals eventually come true.

Splendid with Victory
The Executive Director of the East Region of Taoyuan
Yi-Hung (Tony) Hsu（許翊弘）

Posted on Facebook, "One has to distinguish whether it is a general need or whether the need is mine. The need usually begins generally, and then becomes mine in the end."

Perhaps this is Yi-Hung's version of his mindset or perhaps he's just "postulating".

Yi-Hung was born in Kaohsiung, grew up in Taoyuan, studied in Taipei and served his mandatory military service on Matsu Island.

Where is he from? The best answer to this is: Taiwan.

The most common scene from Yi-Hung's childhood was moving.

His family had no regular residence and their parents changed their professions all the time. He set a record spending four years in three different schools.

Accounting, Electronics and Advertising Design could all be considered his major. After retiring from mandatory military service, he worked as a salesperson at Aurora Office responsible for selling office furniture and he set countless sales records. He was able to predict his sales, not only every month, but for the following six months. The sales for the entire year were under his control. He set goals and realized them. He developed many clients in the government; the most impressive case was the carpeting of Terminal II of the Chiang Kai-shek International Airport. He defeated all other furniture companies and "well-known" salesmen with years more experience and contacts than he had.

What was his secret? He put himself in his client's shoes and pre-considered and analyzed every step for his clients. He even projected better than his clients did, due to his detailed analysis and perfectionism.

He earned more than NT$1 million in his first year working. He said he had the talent of always knowing where to make the sales and to find money-he could "smell" it. However, he quit his well-paid job after only two years to become an apprentice in a computer company to be paid only NT$6,000 (US200) a month because he wanted to study and learn all aspects and practical details of this new industry.

You might think that money wasn't an issue for Yi-Hung. On the contrary, he enjoyed making money. His strategy was to work to learn and then invest. He achieved his skill and experience through working and made his fortune through investing.

His youth was a very enriching time period.

However, one never knows what tomorrow will bring. Over time, the money earned through investing in internet coffee shops, black tea shops and furniture stores was gone through mismanagement and outright betrayal from dishonest business partners. He rapidly learned the principle "Easy come! Easy go!" concerning money.

Yi-Hung decided to reorganize and figure out a new direction for his life and began devoting himself more to religious service. He discovered that God helps those who help themselves and spent a lot of time studying the holy book and practicing its virtues. As a result of this immersion in study and reflection, learning soon became his passion. His greatest comprehension was, **"The greatest method of learning consists of manifesting one's bright virtue."**

The truths of life taught to him by his teachers from an early age, through elementary school and junior high school, up to now had been seen by him as merely material for exams. Now he finally understood the need to apply the knowledge he had learned.

Yi-Hung asked himself what kind of environment he wanted to provide for his two sons. He decided to he wanted them to be able to live happily and to know the basic principles of greatness. For Yi-Hung, life was too serious and complicated. The pursuit of happiness is as simple as creating an environment where children can learn, develop and explore. That was far more valuable than any material fortune.

Occasionally he was invited to meetings of a business referral platform. The culture of this organization is that "givers gain". He noticed the appearance on people's faces and saw that they were excited, cheerful and contented. He knew at that moment that this was the business environment he had been looking for. He invested his savings in a franchise in the eastern area of Taoyuan and began his career as a full-time "giver".

He has been cultivating this referral business for more than two years and he has helped many members find their own direction and correct strategies for life and business and set a successful model for the next generation.

He has helped his members with the skills and knowledge he has accumulated throughout life and has doubled or even tripled his members' businesses. Though still far from a heroic accomplishment, what he has achieved is "arriving at the greatest good". He knows he is moving in the right direction and will persist. According to the law of reciprocation "Givers will eventually gain and meditate in wisdom". And he will continue to persist for he knows there is no end to success. What he cares is not a huge amount of members. What he wants is to build strong teams which there are only cooperation without competition.

Meditate in wisdom.

Postulate for success.

The legend of Yi-Hung is about to begin!

Healthy Baking
The Sensational Happiness
Meng-Yu Chang（常孟渝）

Healthy and simple baking brings the sensation of happiness.

Meng-Yu says, "There is not so much difference between humans and animals."

Being human, the biggest different between humans and beasts is our humanity. If we lose our humanity and act like beasts, we don't deserve to be called human. Sometimes people behave worse than beasts, for they do not have the wisdom to tell right from wrong.

Food safety causes a storm of agitated, angry consumers. Such inhuman conduct by food providers makes us feel aggrieved and infuriated by this society. We do not understand how and why such a lack of conscience can occur over and over again and yet our government and politicians have barely done anything to prevent this from happening.

It could be that the simplicity of life has been complicated by humans in this world. Companies add chemical scents and colors such as clouding agents and plasticizers in order to add flavor to food or to improve the appearance of the original product just to make them sell better.

Apart from being greedy, we often consider ourselves clever. Yet, is a food made of chemicals healthy for human beings? If we feed our livestock chemicals and then eat them for food, where is the logic and sense behind that? What can we do? What can be improved by our newly elected politicians?

What we can do depends on ourselves. We are responsible for seeking and finding the flavor of our conscience.

After Meng-Yu graduated from the Food Processing Department of National Yuanlin Agricultural and Industrial Vocational High School she worked at a bakery for five years and in a hotel for eleven years after that. In between she became acquainted with Executive Chef Yang-Bin Xu and the two were married when Meng-Yu was 23 years old.

Yang-Bin is now the Dean of Hospitality Management Department of Hsing Wu Institute of Technology. The couple cultivates talent and develops new products together. They hope through their efforts they can make people more aware of the value of food hygiene and security.

Most certainly the look and price of food is in disparity with the safety and hygiene of it. Thus, all along the couple has faced many challenges and frustrations. Their goodwill however has had the power to attract people with the same values. Constantly, professional consultants gather together for the same purpose-**to respect food and**

seek to instill humanity.

After years of work, the center of innovative education directed by the couple has finally delivered some positive changes: Natural bread baked with natural yeast and a series of desserts without any flavoring essence or coloring. These products make it possible for the look to follow the simplicity and natural flavor of food. They feel so moved when they see the happy and satisfied smiles on the faces of their customers.

There is joyful news when graduates come back to campus to share their experiences and progress from work. And it is also very comforting to know these graduates are holding on to positive, accurate attitudes in processing the food they sell.

In addition to managing the bakery, Meng-Yu had an opportunity to cooperate with others to produce an original and authentic black soy sauce. To do so she became a farmer in Hualien, planting black soy beans and even brewing them herself. Now the couple has experienced the hard work of being a farmer; including the setbacks such as when their first batch of black soy beans were eaten by barking deer and wild boars. They were so distressed that crying was not enough to relieve their disappointment.

After a few years Meng-Yu finally brewed her first eight jars of soy sauce which passed the strict quality control tests of the Société Générale de Surveillance (SGS) Taiwan. She called them Sauce

Master's Black Soy Sauce, a pure, chemical-free product processed by her own hands-and they danced for joy!

Meng-Yu discovered another truth in making an original natural food and that is: black soy sauce is not actually black. It is the heart of humans who make unsafe food that is black.

The Touch of Coffee
Empathy Brings Fortune
Chung-Hsiu Huang (黃中修)

The fragrance of yellow-brown coffee wafts from the mug.

This is the favorite and best-selling coffee of Chung-Hsiu Huang. When he talks about coffee, Chung-Hsiu will continue his conversation for three days without breaks. He is a young entrepreneur who is addicted to and obsessed by the finest quality coffee beans. He often experiences an "out of stock" supply of them. This made him decide to import them himself and so initiated his venture into the coffee business.

An editor from Min-Shen Newspaper once interviewed a senior Tibetan monk about the heritage of a religious heirloom, the recipe of Putuo Incense. Later the editor was certified as a reincarnation of Rinpoche. This was the mysterious and apparently predestined fate of a member of Chung-Hsiu's family; and this legendary person was his father. It must have been this special background that Chung-Hsiu was born with an innate wit and extra-sensory perception.

During his coffee promoting stage, he discussed the vision of his career with a mother who had an autistic child. The mother shared her worries and frustration with Chung-Hsiu. She had a son around

Chung-Hsiu's age and because of his autism he couldn't find a self-supporting job and wherever he worked, he was easily marginalized. Her son had worked in a relative's company but was laid off without salary after a month because of his "poor performance". Chung-Hsiu could not tolerate this unfairness.

Mindful of his social responsibility, compassion and a desire to help, Chung-Hsiu invited the mother to join his endeavor. "Come and work with me," he said. "I'll open a coffee shop and you and your son can work there…" One month later the shop was opened and business immediately began to sky rocket. The mother was so grateful and thanked him with tears in her eyes. "I didn't think you really meant it! Thank you! Thank you! Thank you!"

That's how Chung-Hsiu's first coffee shop Rising Sun Coffee was founded.

He soon opened a second shop and hired another worker with poor nerve integration. The worker's mother was so touched and grateful that her son had finally found a stable job. As expected, the store is now thriving and prosperous.

Chung-Hsiu learned much from his own acts of benevolence and assistance to these two young disabled men and their anxious mothers. They also helped him to launch his coffee shops and expand his business so that the pleasure of doing business became far more encouraging to him than simply the profit in money.

Chung-Hsiu who graduated from San Francisco State University, loves not only coffee, but also music. He knows how to play the flute and also the violin. He fell in love with musicals after watching Phantom of the Opera and he began researching high quality sound equipment with the help of the father of one of his university classmates.

Chung-Hsiu flavors his coffee with the resonance of music and bakes every single coffee bean with the merging contents of art, happiness, tranquility and elegance. The coffee beans he bakes with these positive qualities and the spirit of, "God helps those who help themselves." He bestows each coffee with a spiritual energy like the sun.

Coffee for Chung-Hsiu delivers a rich fragrance of spirit and blessing. He hopes to warm everyone's heart, body, mind and soul when they drink his coffee, **to make coffee with a Buddha's mind so the fragrance will live on and on.**

I shall not live in vain
A Never Surrender Spirit
Hsing-Hui Huang (黃心慧)

As the poem written by Emily Dickinson:

If I Can Stop One Heart From Breaking

If I can stop one heart from breaking,

I shall not live in vain;

If I can ease one life the aching,

Or cool one pain,

Or help one fainting robin

Unto his nest again,

I shall not live in vain.

Hsing-Hui was deeply influenced by this poem. She has always asked herself. What kind of help she could give to others? How can she make the most and best of her life? What kind of meaning can she "define" her? However, she wants to help more than one heart from breaking. She wants to help the hearts of the world. She was educated in Taiwan and then got a master degree in Advertising Management. Then she founded two English schools, "Princeton Language School" for children and "The World English" for adults. Both of them share the same vision as "Using the beauty of Chinese culture to "have" the heart of the people in the world." Their cultures for them are "BIG". B: Be the cause and benefit others. I: Integrity and inspire. G: Gratitude and give back.

Many Taiwanese people assume that you have to call yourself by a common English name such as Mary, Helen, John or Steven. Actually, the necessity of using an English name has been abused so much! Why do we need English names? These common names are in our ears all the time. The repetitiveness of English names creates a phenomenon in Taiwan. When somebody over the phone says, "Hello! This is Steven." My first response is usually: Steven who?

Chinese people often focus on the meanings and significances of our given names. When children are born, their parents will usually go to a fortune teller for advice about what to name their children. We also change our names to inspire a better destiny. However, we treat our English names so casually.

Forgetting the profoundness of our cultural heritage we put aside the power and meaning inherent in our traditional Chinese characters. We ignore the fact that we are the descendants of the great Yan and Huang emperors. The gifts of our ancestors have become lost and their Great Spirit is dying. Our given name is the first tender, blessing gift of love spoken by our parents. How can we not cherish the voice of love and their calls of expectation?

There are many great English teachers with an excellent capability in English but I admire Hsing-Hui Huang the most. She insists on not calling herself by any other names. She uses the transliteration of her Chinese name-Hsing-Hui Huang and its abbreviation H3. She respects her given name because she respects her parents and she wants to honor them. She is proud that she is Taiwanese.

English is a beautiful language for communication. With the development of modern world history, English is now the International Language. Our purpose for language is to be able to communicate and the purpose of communication is the pursuit of "understanding one another". Before words are transformed into the category of art, we need to know that English is actually a tool for social networking and knowledge of English could be considered one of the most important tools in the world.

However, we really don't need to apologize to foreigners when using English. Usually the first English sentence out of our mouths when we meet a foreigner is "Excuse me, my English is very poor!"

We may not possess such great English ability because we don't use it very often or because we didn't focus on learning it or cultivating our relationships with English in order to become "good friends". We don't make English a part of our lives, or too often, we neglect the ability to connect with the world, which knowledge of English enables us to do. There is nothing wrong with not being able to converse fluently with English. Why do we apologize to foreigners at our first acquaintance? Where does our self confidence go? If they want to be friends with us, they can learn Chinese, too. This was the strong impression H3 left with Hus, Hung after their first conversation. Hus, Hung was touched.

H3 came back to Taiwan after getting her Master's Degree from Michigan State University in the US. She only stayed there two years and she didn't try to look for a job and become an "American" as many students who have studied in America do. She was determined to come back home to Taiwan. With a burning desire in her heart, she knew she had an important mission to accomplish.

H3 desires to help more and more people in Taiwan to know how to use English to attain the level of self-confidence needed to make themselves visible and easily understood. Why should more and more people be good at communicating? Because then we won't have to worry that Taiwan won't be seen by others. We shouldn't wait for odd opportunities such as athletes winning medals in international competitions to hear our national anthem being played and seeing them wave our flag. We should take the initiative and use Chinese culture to conquer the world. With English as a tool, we can show the whole world the strength and depth of our ancient and profound Chinese culture. How can we use English to introduce our long and sophisticated Chinese history and so allow foreigners to share our views? We don't need their sympathy and we shouldn't consider ourselves the weaker.

We should continually make an earnest effort to stand on our own feet and use English to promote and advertise our strengths. We all know the principle that the winner takes it all. So H3 always educates her students to find their own passions and purposes in life and to do their best and then use their advantages in language to honor Taiwan. **What Taiwanese people need is not protection from other countries. What we need is the respect and dignity we can achieve by showing our genuine strengths.** What drives H3 is the burning desire to allow the beauty of Chinese culture and Taiwan to shine and be seen and known by more and more people across the world. That is her mission of love for her motherland.

Above the whiteboard in her English classroom there is an inscription board engraved "Zhuang Yuan" which is the title conferred on the one who came first in the highest imperial examinations of the Qing dynasty. That is a proof of her belief. H3 also loves to share in her love of Chinese culture and the beauty of Taiwan with foreign students and she also loves to share the meanings of Chinese characters. She will explain them to the foreigners she meets in her class and in her life in the hope that they can have a deeper comprehension and identification with Chinese culture and with Taiwan; or better, fall in love with the many aspects of Taiwan life like H3 does.

Even native English speakers are amazed by her ability of simultaneous translation and also by her ability to duplicate the emotional tones of the speakers. She makes communication comprehensible and without boundaries.

In all her years of teaching, H3 never repeats the content of her lectures. Instead she chooses from a breathtaking array of topics, especially aspects of culture and history. All her teaching techniques have impact on her students' ideas about learning a new language. The students advance from simply learning a language to a feast of cultures. No wonder even foreigners can use the phrase, "zhe shi wo de cai" (this is what I desire).

There are claims that she knows little about politics yet she has a deep-rooted and passionate love for her country, for Taiwan is the place where she was nurtured and it is her culture that she wants to honor. Her favorite noun is "Taiwan" and her most passionate verb is "inspire" and the sentence she loves the most is "I come from Taiwan. How may I inspire you?"

The world of English is neither a song nor a slogan. It is a lifetime mission she wants to accomplish. Hsing-Hui Huang is determined to lead all with the vision **to use English to conquer the world and to use culture to permeate people's hearts.**

Hence it is said, "**The world is as infinite as your heart can reach.**"

Essential Love
The Aromatherapy Trainer
Yen-Kai Huang（黃彥凱）

Yen-Kai has worked as manager of IAA (International Association of Aromatherapy) and he has multiple certificates, including Levels 1&2 NAHA of America certificates, ICIM Australia certificate, INHA America certificate and a certificate for Senior Aroma Therapist of China. More so, he is a certified hypnotist by the TMTS Association of America. He is currently the President of AFA, Lohas Association and also the Aromatherapy Training Manager for Mireya

One might ask the question, "Did Yen-Kai have this plan from the beginning?" The answer is, of course not.

Yen-Kai graduated from the Department of International Trade of CYCU which has nothing to do with aromatherapy. He even once thought that aroma oil would blow up like gasoline if exposed to flame. But after hearing a speech, by chance, about aroma oil he accepted the lecturer's guidance and used it to heal an allergic respiratory problem that had been bothering him for a long time. Consequently, his attitude began to change markedly. As he continued to experiment with the aroma oils, unexpected emotions began to surface, his earlier dispassionate rationality began to shift and for the first time, the opinions of others were accepted into his mind. This previously detached and taciturn man became increasingly interested in other people and so he became happier and more outgoing.

These rapid changes shocked Yen-Kai and he gradually fell in love with aroma oil. Eventually, he turned the love for aromatherapy from a passing interest into a career. And so Yen-Kai began his search for any and all courses on the subject of aromatherapy and he began studying everything on the subject he could find.

During his studies, Yen-Kai met a man named Yu-hsian who would later become his instructor and good friend. Yu-hsian provided the help and opportunities that would rocket Yen-Kai's improvement from Earth to Mars and which subsequently led him to the stage of becoming an aromatherapy lecturer.

There was one winter day when Yen-Kai and some others from the association attended an event called "Fine Dinner with the Elders" hosted by the OFO Foundation in northeast Taiwan. The wet and cold winter weather of Keelung was uncomfortable but there were still over thirty senior citizens gathered, waiting for the event. Yen-Kai felt very grateful as he prepared his presentation. He and three other were asked to assist some of the elderly people. One of them chatted with Yen-Kai passionately as if they were friends who had not seen each other for a long time. The elderly woman told Yen-Kai about her son who had left her to live alone and about her husband who had already passed away and she told him stories about her young and wild days. She kept recalling the memories until tears fell from her eyes.

Yen-Kai suddenly thought of his own grandparents back in his hometown and he wondered how much time there was left for him to spend with them. So he picked a day to visit them. He took out the aroma oil which he always carried with him and showed them its magic. After dropping some of the different aroma oils together-lavender, rosemary, orange and sandalwood and shaking and blending them together, he gently massaged them into their necks, shoulders and hands. **His grandmother closed her eyes, filled with the happiness of reunion with her grandson who had disappeared from lives for decades until now. Her tender smile radiated great satisfaction and happiness.**

Yen-Kai made a gift of that bottle of blended aroma oil to his grandmother because she said it smelled so good. He told her to use a few drops when she thinks of him and rub it into her hands. Closing her eyes and taking a deep breath, she could sense her grandson right by her side just like magic. Yen-Kai whispered in his mind, "Don't worry, granny, I'll be back soon to massage your neck and shoulders again, because you're the most important person to me."

Eventually, he had to leave due to his schedule and Yen-Kai waved goodbye to his grandparents, looking expectantly toward his next visit to see his grandmother and they both wept quietly because neither could be sure when it would be.

"The tree wants silence but the wind grants none. The children beg for time but the parents couldn't wait for them."

The most important lesson for Yen-Kai during this time was that one should cherish what one has. Furthermore, he found out the true mission of an aroma therapist is not just the blending the best recipe, but the delivery of love.

Conquering the World
Learn More and Earn More
Feng-Sheng Huang（黃豐盛）

Bald, energetic and optimistic are the first impressions Feng-Sheng imparts to others.

He has cycled and climbed many of the mountain peaks of Taiwan. He has challenged himself by competing in marathons and in the Ironman Triathlon. He has trained himself to be fluent in foreign languages.

He could be described as talented and knowledgeable.

He is a business professional and has a strong business background with an EMBA degree. The secret behind his success is his athleticism and his daring to challenge himself. He reads a lot and diligently practices different languages to strengthen his intellect. He is endowed with civil and mental virtues.

When he was a university student, he wanted to get rich quick because the pay at part-time jobs in restaurants or convenience stores was too low to satisfy him. Therefore, when his classmates introduced him to MLM (Multi-Level Marketing) he thought he had found the shortcut to his success. Consequently, he stocked up on lots of MLM products. It was not until he was discharged from his two years of active military service that he and his family cleared all these wasted goods out of his home.

He was hurt both financially and emotionally. He felt sorry for his family and had learned an expensive lesson: **there is no such a thing as a get-rich-quick opportunity.**

After he left mandatory military service, he worked at a power point consulting firm. The general manger, Xin-Sen Yu made his fortune scolding and yelling at his subordinates. He always scolded and seldom praised anyone. The only compliment Feng-Sheng remembered ever receiving from Xin-Sen was:**"Feng-Sheng, your only advantage is that you are willing to listen to scolding."**

Xin-Sen's standard operating procedure of yelling at and cursing his subordinates was the "training tool" he used to develop customers; rotating, promoting and leading his subordinates without discrimination. Despite the curses, Feng-Sheng managed to be promoted to a million-dollar annual salary.

He later realized that these experiences were to transform and improve his ability.

A crouching tiger of expectation in disguise, the mindset of tough training can turn iron into forged steel.

During his career, Xin-Sen became Feng-Sheng's most cherished advisor but left him with an unfavorable influence. Feng-Sheng had copied Xin-Sen's scolding style. He used this style freely, but many of his coworkers could neither appreciate nor tolerate the constant tongue lashing. Of course, he did occasionally balance his temper to use more refined leadership skills as well.

In 2008, Feng-Sheng partnered with some of his old colleagues to start a new company where he would become his own boss. After two and half years of hard work, their company started to break even and even make some profits. However, conflicts began to emerge caused by his style of management and soon the direction of their company became divided, with one party tending to be more moderate and the other much more "radical".

To resolve this dilemma, Feng-Sheng decided to go it alone and founded EverFortune International Management Consultants Ltd. in 2011. EverFortune International is a professional management consulting firm consisting of accountants, senior bank officers and professional financial planners. They specialize in setting up offshore companies, planning for taxes, developing cross-border investment, and consulting on projects. Most importantly they provide medium-sized and smaller enterprises with the ability and expertise to be able to connect with international markets-a very critical step for enterprises to become part of the world.

Vita Tang is Feng-Sheng's classmate and also his girlfriend. She cherishes every minute of her life because she did not have a smooth childhood. Many of her loved ones died one after the other. She always reminds Feng-Sheng to consider every new day as the last day of his life and not to hesitate in making decisions, to be aggressive and to take action! Vita has been the most influential female in Feng-Sheng's life except for his mother.

Actually Feng-Sheng is naturally aggressive and sometimes seems to be too impatient and impulsive. This is a common challenge for many athletes as they have too much energy without being able to vent it-it's always circling inside their bodies. Fortunately, Feng-Sheng entered a business social network group and he learned to begin every task with the intention of "assisting first" and used this to change his temper to patience. In cooperation and collaboration with the team, he has learned that it takes a consensus to cooperate and with common understanding with everybody on the team. With this, reaching their goals is guaranteed and nobody needs to ever yell or scold.

If an industry wants to be seen in the world, the fastest way is to set up a company in the country you want to enter and promote the product locally. That is the most dependable and feasible business model. However, to be able to do so you need an experienced, faithful and dependable vanguard to assist you in handling all the minor details. Feng-Sheng is your best choice.

If you have Feng-Sheng to help you with offshore development, you will smoothly conquer the world.

The Chi-gong Master
Selfless Sharing
Chih-Ming Peng（彭智明）

The myth that Peng-tsu lived for 800 years is no rumor. For if one practices Chi and mind with wisdom, one's energy will eventually flow with light.

Chinese culture is deep and profound but the legacy lessens with each passing generation. It would be boasting to simply brag about one's history but honoring one's ancestors by learning their wisdom has always been a far better way.

Peng-tsu lived for so long-800 years-that his knowledge and wisdom still shines in modern days. His offspring dedicated their lives to promoting selflessness just like their ancestor himself loved and helped people in ancient times.

Many consider that the tale of Peng-tsu was no more than a myth, but he truly existed. Hoping to benefit others, his descendants accumulated his wisdom to share with the world. Instead of keeping the knowledge for themselves they allowed people whose destiny was linked together to understand the true road to health and longevity. The offspring of Peng-tsu is Chih-Ming Peng, founder of the Peng style of Chi-gong.

Two years ago, the first time I met Master Peng (Chih-Ming) in person, both of us high-fived like old friends. At that very moment, a flow of energy from his palm poured into and sped through my entire body. The shock I experienced at that moment has been the reason why I maintained such a close friendship with him. And that positive energy is still flowing in my veins and muscles, pumping every part of me, keeping me energetic.

Ancient peoples practiced chi-gong and martial arts for health alone whereas modern people do so in order to fight. If one carries impure thoughts when practicing any martial arts, he will eventually walk the wrong path. And once he starts down that path, evil thoughts will begin to corrode his mind, eventually causing him to harm others.

Therefore, Master Peng preaches that practicing chi-gong is actually training one's mind, similar to penance, and once mind and chi synchronize, body and thoughts achieve balance. One will discover true peace and will be able to conquer any obstacle and achieve any goal.

Everyone desires the luck to have every wish come true, but normally in vain because normal people are too weak in their minds and in their will. They differ from successful people who are hard-working and energetic all the time but if one trains his mind and chi very well, not only will his body become stronger, but so shall his concentration and will strengthen up, too.

Therefore, **Master Peng stated the three necessities of life: peaceful mind, healthy body and right living. These three things combined together, are the training of will.**

In June 2010, Master Peng transformed his family-only martial arts style into a series of simple fitness drills and founded the Peng-style of Chi-gong. Practitioners are able to form their bodies into the perfect instrument for carrying out the will by releasing wasted chi, producing a finer chi and gathering purified chi. Then one can accomplish anything in his mind.

The Ancient Chinese people were usually very interested in teaching their wisdom, but ironically they also tended to withhold the ultimate of their knowledge in order to protect themselves from being defeated by their apprentices. Therefore, much profound ancient wisdom and skill was forgotten and became lost and eventually vanished from the minds of men and finally became only a myth.

But Master Peng broke this habit and instead passed down all of his family secrets to his students using modern technology such as digital photographs, audio recordings and even videos because he wants the knowledge of his ancestors to last forever as a living legend instead of as an ancient myth.

The students and apprentices of Master Peng are so multitudinous and diverse, they reside in every part of the world and because the teaching is done in the International Language of English, Master Peng has not only Chinese students but also students of other ethnicities as well, which speaks volumes of his vision to embrace the whole world.

His many students include celebrities in politics and business and can be represented by his recent invitation to speak to China's elite leadership group, Zhenghe Island. But Master Peng would not speak about his success, fame and impact because he understands the wisdom to view life without cares. "To take is to gather chi while to lay is to release." Even a simple quote can show his wisdom from practicing Chi-gong and martial arts.

Master Peng reminds us to not practice too long-a quarter of an hour every day is enough. The real important thing is to focus on the flow of chi and empty one's mind in order to quickly and effectively enhance one's concentration. **If one practices Chi-gong correctly, intently, happily and wisely it won't take too much hard work to live a brilliant life.**

Undefeated Real Estate Tycoon
Po-Hong Ku（辜博鴻）

It was the anniversary day of the May Fourth Movement and also the birthday of Matsu (Goddess of the Sea). Po-Hung's mother was busy preparing for the ceremony and the hard physical work caused her to go into premature labor. It was three months ahead of his expected due date. Growing up in the fishing village of Badou Zi in Keelung, his life was full of adventures and many ups and downs.

In the living room of their home, there were certificates and awards everywhere for his brothers' and sisters' stellar academic achievements. By contrast, the only prize he ever won during his elementary school years was an attendance award. He was neither the most intelligent nor the most athletic and taught himself at a young age to accept the feeling of being ignored by his family.

In order to reduce his family's financial burden, he joined the military for eight years, after graduating from the Keelung Electrical Branch of Commerce and Industry. After retiring from military service, he started a business selling model Pagodas. During this time period, he met his wife Xiao-Ling and had a son and a daughter. He made some money at the beginning and invested in real estate, which unfortunately led them into a wretched situation. They were short of cash and the checks they wrote started bouncing. It was a frightening situation for them both. They had to take several jobs at the same time but nothing was more important than earning enough to support their family. Po-Hung worked at hotels helping people park their cars and he also drove a taxi. Xiao-Ling sold clothes on the side of the road. They would do anything necessary, within reason, to make their money. Their greatest blessing was "only" having two other part-time jobs. Looking back at what they had been through during that period would bring tears to their eyes. It was one of the hardest times of their lives.

Po-Hung learned a lifelong lesson from this experience. He recognized that his failure had come from not having the concepts of living within his means and of risk assessment. He began to study financial management and started working at an investment consulting company. He comprehended the principles of leveraging and founded an organization call "Rich Dad". He also began to get involved in current public and social services. Along with his personal growth, he accumulated a wealth of knowledge and became an expert in resource integration and asset management.

During the period of SARS in Taiwan, there was a tremendous panic in the real estate industry. Investors were eager to sell and Po-Hung and his wife chose to buy. They earned their first pot of gold with that investment and began to turn their lives around.

With the money they earned, Po-Hung stepped out and founded the Ling Chun Resource Integration Company in 2004.

Po-Hung's company targeted management of suites which were considered less profitable by others in real estate but which were relevant to services for his clients. His "blue ocean strategy" was to face the most unwanted tasks and turn trash into gold. He was inspired by the moral: **"Don't behave with wickedness because it seems insignificant. Don't neglect a good deed because it seems insignificant." He converted this into "Don't invest just because of the huge profit. Don't neglect to invest just because of the tiny profit."** He extends this concept to the example of drinking straws. The profit is so little that no-one wants to manufacture them. However, the demand for straws is huge because almost everyone needs one. Those who invested in manufacturing straws made a huge amount of money. Those who just observed without action could only swallow their regret. The theory of "many small drops make an ocean" contributed to the legend of Po-Hung's Suites Management.

Many outmoded apartments were waiting for the chance to be renovated but were pending on the market and were empty. Po-Hung remodeled them and transformed their appearance. He repackaged them and sent them out, not only preserving the company's value but also increasing its revenue.

Po-Hung created a systematic management method for renting

suites by reducing risks and avoiding argumentative tenants who won't pay rent or worse, murder their landlords. On the other hand, students who study away from home, people who leave their home town or people who can't afford to buy houses or apartments-all of these people have had unhappy experiences renting. The service Po-Hung's provides is a solution to all troubles encountered in renting, such as substandard treatment or harassment from landlords. Tenants and landlords together are taken care of and they both feel satisfied and comfortable. It is a perfect, flawless and bidirectional service which is totally undefeatable.

Results speak louder than words and the achievements of Ling Chun Link Rich Resource Integration Company are leagues ahead of their competition. His company is the leading business model in his industry. They own branches in Northern, Central and Southern Taiwan with more than 70 people currently queuing for services. Their outstanding performance comes from the benevolence and vision of Po-Hung.

Now Po-Hung is ready to expand his outstanding system globally. He wants people across the world to witness and benefit from their endurance and persistence and to embrace their ideal and vision.

A letter sent to his wife one sultry midnight while exploring and developing markets in Cambodia, sums up his success: "Dear Xiao-Ling, Thank you for all your love and support over these many years. I credit you for all of our lifetime achievements. It is your companionship and contribution that has made this possible. Thank you."

Husband and wife, working together with calloused hands and blistered feet, finally achieve their dream. Cherish and treasure.

A Legend from Mount Chilai
No. 1 Oolong Tea Ambassador
Yin-Shan Tang（湯尹珊）

It was like a mandate from heaven ever since Yin-Shan Tang was born. You can tell her mission from her name. She is the worldwide ambassador for Taiwan's Oolong tea.

Longjing and Pu'er come from far away where JinXuan and Oolong grow on the mountain peaks. It doesn't matter what kind of tea you are making, they are all remedies for anxiety.

"The Benefit of Tea" is a song written in 1995 that has been regarded as a song for tea houses ever since. The author has made intensive study and accumulated profound knowledge of tea. However, when the tea-infatuated author met Yin-Shan, he was impressed and touched. Not only does she possess exquisite taste in the qualities of tea but she also has a strong sense of obligation about disseminating Taiwanese tea culture to every corner of the world. Four of her family members have devoted their lives to the leading the promulgation of the history of Oolong tea. **Not many people are so acquainted with tea, but Yin-Shan's family are a rarity. They are especially knowledgeable in "High Mountain Oolong Tea".** Yin-Shan's grand grandfather started planting Assam Black Tea in Yuchih

County, Nantou in 1950. That was the origin of tea growing for the Tang, more than sixty years ago.

Taiwan's export market shrank immediately following World War II and the tea growing business was practically forgotten until 1982 when the government began a specific policy of promoting tea growing. This gave a new lease of life to tea growers. Yin-Shan's father Tang, Wen initiated the growing of High Mountain Oolong and waited until 1988 to have their first harvest. It was the beginning of restoring the glory of tea.

Tang, Wen was concerned about who could be the successor to his tea business and able to manage the transformation of a tradition-bound industry. This question had long bothered him along with the other traditional industry owners. Tang, Wen's children had finished their studies and decided to return to take up the baton of their family tea industry. They would continue to cultivate the spirit of Taiwan's tea culture. What a touching scene it was for their father to be able to witness the participation of the new younger generation of tea growers.

Yin-Shan's younger brother Chia-Hung's majored in Computer Science and Information Engineering and he utilized his knowledge to improve the arts of tea processing. He went up to Mount Chilai to examine the details of planting, picking, selecting, processing and baking tea. He applied his knowledge and technology to control fermentation and the heat of baking and recorded all procedures in detail.

Chia-Hung clearly knows that the technology used in baking is critical to the uniqueness, redolence and flavor of the tea. Additionally, Chia-Hung researched the different serving functions of tea sets. Paying such attention to detail with a combination of traditional and scientific thinking has been a bit peculiar. However, this kind of self-meditation has led her to be able to come up with many unique marketing strategies in promoting the ancient culture of tea to the modern world.

Yin-Shan selected the Promotion of Agriculture when studying for her degree from the Department of Natural Resources at Chinese Cultural University. The subject aroused her interest in agriculture and she continued her studies by obtaining her Master's Degree in Agricultural Extension at National Taiwan University. After graduating, she worked at the Agricultural Extension Center and Academia Sinica.

During this period, she studied in Canada for one year and with her brought printed pamphlets about Taiwan, along with a whole set of tea pots and cups and home-grown tea harvested from her father's farm. She never overlooked the fact she was from Taiwan and promoted Taiwan culture at every opportunity. Her time in Canada awakened her ardent love for Taiwan's tea. After returning from Canada, Yin-

Shan went home and took charge of the family business with her younger brother. She tried to figure out how to promote their brand of Taiwan Oolong tea to the whole world. She knew that lacking a proper marketing strategy, no matter how outstanding the products are, they will remain unknown and unwanted. Yin-Shan didn't want to create an image based only on the fleeting curiosity some Europeans and Americans have for Taiwanese tea. That would be far too superficial. This is similar to seeing awkward Chinese characters in tattoos printed on foreigners. What she wanted to focus on was the quality aspect of High Mountain Oolong from Taiwan. Her desire was to hear the sound of "Wow!" and to see the thumbs up gesture when people tasted their brand.

She insists on maintaining the highest possible quality of their product. Quality control starts from their own tea gardens. They plant, pick, and bake all the tea by themselves and their farmers have won numerous awards and have received Council of Agriculture Traceability Certification. Integrity and trustworthiness is their commitment.

Yin-Shan founded TeaTalk Academy and she seeks to expand their dimensions. Since opening, the school's fame has spread far and wide. Her goal is to attract people to Taiwan to learn more about Taiwan's Oolong tea industry. If you wanted to know the ancient wine-growing traditions of France, you would go to the vineyards, visit their wine cellars, listen to their stories, touch the oaken barrels, witness the aging marks and soak yourself in the wine-growing atmosphere in order to really experience the exclusive mellow quality of the wines. When we hear of "sandalwood" we think of East India. When we see roses, we think of Bulgaria. When we smell jasmine, we think of "Cleopatra". When we think of tea, Yin-Shan's vision is that people think of Taiwan.

Across the world there is a kind of tea that can shake the universe, inspire people and enlighten and enliven their body, mind and spirit. You can drink it, admire it, smell and listen to it. We will leave the explanations to Yin-Shan and let her tell you the story.

She says, **"Drink the high mountain tea grown in the clouds in Taiwan and distribute Oolong tea to every corner of the world."**

Steadfast and Preserving
The Executive Director of Kaohsiung
Chi-Fu (Kevin) Yang（楊啓富）

In just 5 months there are now over 83 members in the FuLe Platinum Chapter in the Hall of Fame in Kaohsiung in Taiwan. We couldn't imagine how majestic the chapter would be created at its official launch on the ninth of June of 2015. However we can be sure of one thing. Kevin (Chi-Fu) Yang has definitely broken the "world record" for the number of members at the launching of a BNI chapter. This explosive growth power comes from the harsh challenges of his experiences in life.

Kevin Yang, the executive director of Kaohsiung Region, is the protagonist of our story.

Kevin was born in a prosperous family in Tainan. Unfortunately, his father went bankrupt during a recession of the construction industry. They even lost their house because it was foreclosed by the bank. It was another practical case in our book, one falls from Heaven to Earth.

Kevin suffered under the impact of the recession and chose to major in Industrial Economics at Tamkang University wishing he could figure out the reason why his family business had collapsed.

This period was the lowest and the most difficult time in his life. He paid his tuition through student loans and did a lot of part-time jobs. He worked at different factories as a laborer, he delivered lunch boxes, worked in tea stores served at school and did telephone cold calling.

He filled up his time with work. Why? He knew he must depend on himself and persist to live up to his best. Though he was busy and his schedule packed, he still joined a Kendo club to test his focus and to be steadfast and persevering through all the hard practice. He is grateful to his high school classmate Zhao-Hong Lin. Zhao-Hong gave him the most needed support and help at the toughest time in his life. That was a wonderful and true experience of accountability and a gift of timely assistance.

Zhao-Hong was indeed an invaluable friend who helped when he needed it most. During that challenging time any type of entertainment was very much a luxury for Kevin. However, he would choose to watch some motivating movies to inspire and encourage himself. He learned and saved up his fighting power.

The most touching movie for Kevin was The Pursuit of Happiness. Kevin asked himself with tears covering his face. "When will happiness knock on my door?" "Should I go out to search for my own true happiness?"

As a consequence, traveling is now his favorable hobby. He loves to travel to relax and expand his horizons and cultivate different aspects about life. He has been to almost everywhere in the world. Still, his home country of Taiwan is still his favorite. Kevin has a younger brother who has a mental disability.

When asked whether Kevin loves his brother or not. Kevin replied with certainty. He even used his pay from his first part time job to buy gifts for him. Kevin loves his only brother and he considers his brother's future his responsibility. He loves to find the proper time to hug him and tell his brother sincerely. "I love you. I'll keep company with you. You are great and brave and I'm proud of you." This kind of love touched us.

There is a story about Thomas Edison, when his factory was destroyed by fire and reduced to ashes after an explosion. Every worker was informed and gathered at the site of the accident. They were all frightened about the accident and worried about their future. Edison gave a speech in front of the destroyed factory.

A similar incident happened to Kevin. One night in 2013 Kevin was on his way to a meeting with members of BNI from Vietnam to exchange knowledge. When he drove to the parking gate of the restaurant, his car suddenly caught on fire. He escaped from his burning car filled with panic

Staring at his burning car, the story of Edison's popped into his mind. He had a sudden recognition that this was a blessing in disguise and he would rebuild his own correct and reliable transportation (methodology) to be able to reach his destination (goals) safely.

He knew that he needed to have a more stable system to help himself and the people he cared for to become successful. He then became the executive director of BNI Kaohsiung.

He got everything ready and set out to recruit members and began setting up chapters at lightning fast speed.

He attracted entrepreneurs to join him with his enthusiastic, sincere and hard-working personal quality. Holding the same vision and burning with the passion of Southern Taiwan, embracing the industriousness needed to flip the situation and treating each other with sincere brotherhood; a legend was formed in launching a new chapter with such a bountiful number of members for BNI.

For Kevin, it is a matter of responsibility and commitment. This brilliant achievement is just the beginning of Kevin's success and he is grateful to every attendee.

He says: "When happiness knocks, I won't say I am not there. When opportunity meets success, I am prepared." We asked why Kevin called his chapter FuLe (Wealthy and Happy). Kevin explained, "Poverty won't bring happiness; wealth doesn't guarantee happiness, either. I am hoping to bring material abundance, success and happiness to all aspects of our members' lives through real help and cooperation. We will not be troubled by money and we won't be bothered with failure."

Hence it is said: **In the Pursuit of Happiness, FuLe is ready to blossom.**

Messenger of Love
The Executive Director of Tainan City –
Ying-Shun Liao（廖英順）

Who am I? Ying-Shun used 16 A4 sized paper with solid and dense sentences to describe his 48 years journey of life. The author spent 66 minutes with 666 cc. of tears trying to report the touching feelings. When he was young, a fortune teller once told him that no matter how hard he tries, he won't achieve success before the age of 52.After 52, all the hindrances and obstacles will be gone and his achievement will come eventually. How can a man full of youthful vigor take that advice and believe in it? He was a genius born in a blue collar family with 6 brothers and sisters in Taipei. His parents did not have any particular cultivating plan for any of their children. However, he was very diligent and anything he read he could record and remember like a scanner; and then, categorize all the data into his brain. After he observed the information, he could apply them with his own innovation and creativity. Before he graduated from high school, he went to the National Museum of History for a painting exhibition. It was his hobby in his leisure time. He ran into Master Lin Yun (a well known fortune teller in Taiwanese history). When one of the female pupils of Lin Yun approached him and told him that Master Lin Yun wanted to read his fortune. He was surprised and a bit astonished and the Master said to him, "You should study hard. One day you will be very famous. But you are facing a disaster right now. I want to teach you how to get through the hidden barrier. Since I am leaving for America tomorrow, you can go to one of the teachers at your school. I will ask him to pass on the doctrine to you."

He did accordingly and because of this doctrine, it cured his unknown headache and helped him through the pressure of taking the entrance exam for university. He was able to get into his ideal department and school: Department of Architecture of National Cheng Kung University.

This story was revealed at one of the chats he had with his mother. His mother told him that he fell down and passed out for more than a week. His mother went to a temple and prayed for the extension of his life. The God in the temple did some magic and said this magic could only protect Ying-Shun until 18. The year Ying-Shun met Master Lin Yun, he turned 18. The appearance of Master Lin Yun extended his life of wisdom. He was touched and was grateful about the rescue. After that conversation with his Mom, he believed in karma and fate. He did not dare to be rash and his adventure to find the purpose of life began.

If studying is his specialty then art is his interest. He is clever at arts and crafts, painting and calligraphy. Not to mention his major, architectural design. Ying-Shun was addicted to books. He would read whatever books in front of him. He took a part time job working in the university library and never let any books slip by. He soaked himself into the sea of knowledge. His misfortune began after he graduated and became a white collar worker in the society. He set out as an interior designer and took the advice of his clients and became the owner of a restaurant.He could not attract the clients of other restaurants so his restaurant was empty. He ended up in debt. He tried to make a comeback and did MLM and was trapped in debts again. He went bankrupt this time. He gave himself visions over and over. He tried to overcome them but his nightmares hit him again and again. He was completely defeated by fate. At this stage of life, Ying-Shun began to avoid everything and everyone. He tried to evade responsibility. He didn't want to face the disappointment from his relatives and he was afraid of the demands for repayment of debts from his creditors. He was so depressed and panicked about his future. He wondered about the reason why he had such a tough life. If everyone was born for a purpose then why was he so useless? He even thought about ending his life. However, be recalled the pseudonym "Wei-fan" he used when he was in high school. The meaning of "Wei-fan" in Chinese is a boat. He suddenly realized that the purpose of his life was buried in his subconscious.

"Benefit others with ego" become his guidance for life:

He decided to devote his life to charity and in the process of helping others he found himself and the purpose for his life. In 1996, he signed an agreement for donating his organs and donating his whole body in 2011.He began a life style of delivering love. **He also founded the "Taiwan LifeCare Welfare Association" in 2012; and activated**

his plan for delivering love to help the minority and disabled. Every activity he conducted touched the hearts of everyone.

During all the difficulties and challenging time of his life, he met his current wife Xi Xia Lin.She had a tragic marriage before and had one son and one daughter with her ex-husband.Ying-Shun gave up the concept of having his own children and loved his wife and her children with all his heart and soul.Xi Xia supported him without complaints or regrets.She also honored his dignity carefully. It makes Ying-Shun feel that she is his only love. His wife is the vice president of Lei Shan Insurance and is the cornerstone of Taiwan LifeCare Welfare Association.She supports him and gives him power to promote his idea. Husband and wife work with a concerted effort nothing can hinder them. True love can move all the tough challenges away. Ying-Shun franchised a business network platform with the culture of Givers Gain.The model of this organization was business in accordance with his beliefs. He wanted to find more fellow enthusiasts to spread love and create their own business; and to have feedback to society and benefit others. The law of reciprocation is what Ying-Shun follows. As Michelangelo once said "I do not carve. I just remove the unwanted stone."For Ying-Shun it was "I do not invest. I discover."

Ying-Shun's philosophy of life is identical with the author. Put others benefit before oneself without consideration for oneself. Hence it is: No existence of ego. Altruism is love.

Ying-Shun's life is not in vain.

The Record of Happiness and Blessings
Ivy Bride
Chia-Chin Liao（廖嘉今）

Ivy Bride is located at No. 42, Ai-kuo East Road. It sounds patriotic, but the real story is the miraculous development of Taiwan's wedding photo shooting industry.

In the 1970s, Taiwan was still very innocent. At that time, Chia-Chin Liao's father ran a small grocery store in Rui-fang selling cheap household items, eventually becoming the biggest wholesale center in northern Taipei.

CTV Photo Company was a simple photo studio. The original owner was the inventor of the flexible straw which became so popular that they decided to sell the studio to Chia-Chin's aunt and uncle in 1974. The uncle invited Chia-Chin's father to come and work with him in the photo studio and they ran the business together. Soon Chia-Chin's whole family joined the battlefield, bringing a new era to Taiwan's bridal photography market.

Firstly, to make it easy for couples to get married the studio began renting wedding gowns. Later, make-up and hair styling were added to the project. Such a combination of services was unprecedented at that time.

Chia-Chin's brother laid out a promotional campaign with exquisite designs and advertisements to develop a vision of ceremonial beauty and true happiness. Within a few years, CTV Bridal World had become Taiwan's premier bridal photo company and pioneers in the industry.

Becoming Taiwan's role model wasn't the goal of Chia-Chin's father, he set the stakes higher to become the world's number one; and although in other countries the bridal photo industry was not the same, Taiwan still had to be the leader, making itself a role model for the world.

CTV Bridal Magazine was established with its own art, design and editing teams providing up-to-the-minute details on fashionable wedding designs. It was called the contemporary bible for brides.

Taiwanese opera treasure Li-hua Yang was married in 1983 and she was the first to grace the cover of CTV Bridal Magazine. However, the groom Wen-dong Hung indicated that his part of the service was lacking in efficiency. Grooms weren't being taken care of!

Within six months, the men's Western-style suit department was established and from that time the company continued heading towards greater and finer professionalism. This was the spirit of CTV Bridal World.

According to Taiwanese custom one can only have one wedding, so the same dress cannot be worn twice; and in the past, photos were all shot on the day of the wedding. But how to produce perfection in an age when timing was so vital to everything?

This trial tested the company's wisdom. On a busy day, up to 72 couples could be waiting in line. Photographers and staff barely had time to breathe doing their jobs.

The CTV Bridal team developed a clever explanation: The goddess of brides appears only on the wedding day. If the bridal dress is worn on another day, the bride should not be worried.

This imaginative stratagem resolved the company's tight scheduling and put their clients' minds at ease.

From 1989 the company started shooting photos outdoors.

This was a Taiwanese specialty and the skill of Taiwan's photographers brought other countries' wedding businesses to Taiwan to learn. Foreign couples even came to Taiwan just to have their wedding photos shot outdoors. That was a witness to the economic miracle of Taiwan's bridal industry.

The now famous Korean bridal business modified Taiwan's experiences by adding artistic backdrops as an added feature.

Time changes trends and market status. Following the baby boom of the 1950s and 1960s, the government encouraged married couples to have only two children. Then fewer people got married and the bridal industry struggled with its first setbacks.

After SARS, the whole economic environment changed. The company was handed over to Chia-chin Chia-Chin and she changed its name to Ivy Bride in 2000. Considering fewer people were getting married in Taiwan, Chia-Chin actively developed markets in Hong Kong, Japan, Singapore.

Ivy Bride was a hit at the Hong Kong showcase exhibition and many couples formed groups to come to Taiwan to shoot their bridal photos. On the market they advertise: If you don't come to Taiwan for bridal photos, you are behind the times.

Ivy's competitors became so jealous they even asked the police to intervene!

Their glory days came to an end, however, eight years ago when competitors from mainland China joined the battlefield. They lowered profit margins and flooded the marketplace with cut prices. So, Chia-Chin chose to withdraw.

She had watched the bridal photography business evolve from modest and uncomplicated settings to the utter extravagance and back again over a twenty year cycle.

Looking back on her business, Chia-Chin believes the changes in fashion were not grasped quickly or alertly enough and that this was one of the reasons why Ivy could not surpass the prosperity of CTV.

Chia-Chin Liao is a successful businesswoman, graceful and

generous and Ivy Bride projects the love that every truly happy couple share; and that each picture is a blessing. Their wish is for all couples to have happiness with their wedding photos and in their marriage.

Thus it is said, **"Happy brides are with Ivy; a happiness that is felt all over the world."**

Energetic Happiness Maker
Yung-Chieh Chao（趙詠捷）

Born into a scholar's family, Yung-Chieh had an enviable environment to grow up in. He was provided with a well-planned blueprint for life the moment he was born. Yung-Chieh's nickname is Lele (which means happiness in Chinese) and his elder sister was called Huanhuan (which means cheerful). It is not difficult to figure out that both Yung-Chieh and his sister were well taken care of and his parents had big plans in raising them.

Yung-Chieh was like Dennis the Menace. He was always full of energy. His favorite hobby was playing online video games because he felt by playing in virtual reality he could get hurt and die over and over. Moreover, he could be a superhero. Plus it was a safe game for a seven-year-old boy who had already broken his leg and had to be in a plaster cast for three months.

Yung-Chieh enjoyed himself being creative, setting goals, and challenging himself. It was exciting and provided a way for him to vent his energy. Later in life, he considered himself a specialist in computer engineering. He tried to learn everything relevant to computers. Analogous to the "digital treasures" in a computer game, he would not stop until he made them his own. He collected many of these digital treasures in order to deal with his more tenacious opponents. There was a time, not only in Taiwan but around the world, when every kid was raising an electronic chicken called "Tamagotchi". Yung-Chieh confronted all the many challenges of "Tamagotchi" and completed the procedure in a week. It was a lot faster than raising a real chicken. He set the record and gained a lot of admiration from his classmates. From his experiences in playing on-line games he understood the rapid progress of information technology. And he recognized that if you didn't lead the trend, you will fall behind immediately. So Yung-Chieh majored and specialized in computer science and kept updating his knowledge in the field.

After he graduated from the Department of Information Engineering, he continued his education and received a master's degree in Digital Technology Design (Master's Program in Toy and Game Design). The title of his master's degree mirrored his experience in playing and learning at the same time, balancing between having fun and education. Under his mother's insistence, he first completed his mandatory military service and then went back to school for his master's degree. Yung-Chieh was then able to start working immediately after receiving his master's degree. During this time, he worked in four different companies, two of which offered a very high salary and there was no time lag between jobs. After obtaining the experience he needed, he borrowed NT$100,000 from his parents to start his own company with some friends, but it soon went out of business. He realized that running a business and working for others was totally different; especially when you also have to handle the many problems between business partners.

Destitute people suffer from colds, but so do the rich. Every walk of life has its own trouble. For Yung-Chieh, his biggest challenge was to prove himself. He wanted to be someone and do something to honor his family and to make his parents proud of him. He sometimes forgot he was still young and had a lot of opportunity. He had to accept that there always would always be trials and errors. Failure in business can be a blessing in disguise.

"It was awful tasting medicine but I guess the patient needed it." Steve Jobs once said in a speech to Stanford University graduates.

Yung-Chieh felt beaten and his business failure had hurt his confidence. He was in a dilemma about whether he should remain his own boss or whether to become a worker again. He thought about changing his name to "Mr. Confusion" because he felt he had lost the ability to direct his own life. During this period of depression, his kind and wise English teacher gave him some advice which woke him up from his lethargy. She pointed out to him that he was skilled at computer information systems and setting up and maintaining "connect systems" for his organization. "Many people don't understand the benefits of these systems," she said. "You should take advantage of your professional skills and help other members set up their profiles so they can receive more global exposure. I can help you with the Chinese/English translations."

She reminded him that he was a gifted and talented entrepreneur. "Don't indulge yourself in self-pity. Use your strengths to help those who need it, you should be ashamed for giving up so easily. Be responsible for your own success and confront your fears. Only by helping others first, will your talents be seen."

Yung-Chieh was inspired. Through helping members to expose their excellence through the "Connect System" the distinction of Taiwan's industry could be seen over the world. If he helped enough people to become successful, he would become successful too. And when Taiwan was seen, he would be seen, too.

After hearing her advice, Yung-Chieh pondered the matter the whole night. After that, he mustered his forces and started afresh. He founded a new business and became his own boss. Soon his first order knocked on his door-a 3.5 million dollar (US$117,000) contract for a game design. He felt so relieved that his confidence immediately returned.

In addition to designing on-line games he also helped his fellow members set up their personalized Connect Systems and made them become their own boss.

Happiness has become a reality and he has built his local business into a global network.

The Secret Diary of Liu, NaiBa (Nanny Liu)'s Internet Business
Fang-Yu Liu（劉芳育）

You may not have heard about "Liu Fang Yu". However, if you Google Search "Liu, NaiBa" (Nanny Liu), you will discover a series of related internet websites about his life. The most touching story is the one of how Nanny Liu got started in business. He calls himself "Daddy" so you can imagine this is the story of a man who loves children.

"Three Men and a Baby" is a movie which impresses many people. Yet, such tasks do not baffle Nanny Liu.

His story begins ten years ago when he first took a job selling software for a computer company. At the time he recognized the need to overcome his timidity and fear of strangers but he faced great discouragement when bluntly told by one his supervisor that he was unable to do "cold calls." The supervisor told Nanny Liu, "You have such a terrible sales record, being in sales is obviously not a suitable profession for you!"

Such a nullification of his ability reduced his esteem and self-confidence and for a moment he felt that this would be a major failure in his career. But he refused to accept this person's conclusion. Instead he found his own style of acquainting himself with his customers.

He gathered e-mail addresses from several company information departments and began to introduce himself and share experiences he had gained from his work with the customers he had contacted previously. Weeks went by and finally he received a reply from one of his customers. He said he liked this kind of sharing and he found the stories inspiring and interesting. The two struck a chord with each other.

As the months went by, many customers began to feel the connection and became willing to learn more about Nanny Liu's products. Some of them even took the initiative to invite Nanny Liu to their company to introduce his products personally. His supervisor was surprised at the courteous reception he received when going with Nanny Liu to present their company products. He was curious, "Are you close to these people?"

Nanny Liu responded, "No. We met for the first time today."

Through this experiences and training, Nanny Liu discovered he had an unusual talent. He was able to open people's hearts with his words. His confidence returned and a few months later, he founded his own business.

Using the best of his expertise he set up his own web-site. He bought a product called "Easily Set Up a Web-Site and Manage E-mails" and brought it home. After studying it carefully, he compared all competing products currently on the market and listed "50

Questions & Answers" concerning product usage and then provided his own solutions and posted them on his web-site. The 50 Q&A's were an immediate hit and were visited more than a thousand times and he received many phone calls asking for his personal advice. He knew that he was onto something.

In 2006, the usage of blog marketing became very popular. Internet entrepreneurs began spontaneously appearing on the market. It took only a very low threshold to brand a new product. One needed only to take some photos and write an article about them. Riding this trend Nanny Liu wrote more than fifty serial articles about his own story in founding his career. He shared his most stimulating and thought-provoking incidents from his experiences dealing with his customers.

His first story coincided with the birth of his first child and he completed all ensuing stories while taking care of him. In his blog, he recorded his personal stories of founding a business and raising a child, so he named the blog "The Secret Diary of Nanny Liu's Internet Business."

It was a gift for his first son and it brought them both widespread acclaim and popularity. Even the well-known writer Ruo-Quan Wu invited Nanny Liu onto his radio program at the Broadcasting Corporation of China to share his experiences from his career on the internet.

From that point on he was invited to give speeches at schools, public agencies and on other radio programs. Nanny Liu began to taste success.

It was Nanny Liu's expertise to narrow the distance between people through his articles. However, he soon began to sense an unreality and emptiness imposed by constantly writing without direct human touch or contact.

With this realization he decided to join a platform for referrals and began cooperating with other businessmen and entrepreneurs to widen his network and create more creative opportunities for himself.

We all know you can't get a haircut through the internet. Trust and human contact can't be achieved through the internet alone.

Later Nanny Liu was asked to speak at the Chinese Lecturers Union. He met quite a few professional speakers and began to assist them to set up and maintain their own personal websites. This was the opportunity he had longed for. He knows that internet business no longer consists only of cold computers. Internet business is a combination of internet and social networking at a global level.

Gratitude for the Real Benefactor
Giving and Becing
Bang-Ning (Simon) Liu（劉邦寧）

Simon (Bang-Ning) Liu is the most humble senior the author has ever known. There's so much more to him than first meets the eye. He talks little of the skills and talent he has accumulated over the six decades of productive life. During that time he has amassed an impressive array of knowledge. He has earned three Masters Degrees and one PhD.

Notwithstanding this remarkable academic achievement, Simon never stops learning and cultivating further knowledge. His unfathomable mien, like that of a KungFu master, belies his scholastic achievements and abundant wealth of professional experience. Such is its scope that his job record could not be covered in three pages-not to mention his achievements in travel, reading, networking and music, which are some of his pastimes. He enjoys listening to all styles and genres of music. He exemplifies the idea that although knowledge may be found in books experience is found only in living.

He also gifted in the most remarkable art of reading minds. Simon has an extra-sensory perception that makes it possible for him to know one's thoughts after little more than a simple conversation and he continues to cultivate this ability through meeting countless people in his experiences and travels.

It's difficult to imagine that this modest gentleman had such an extraordinary childhood background.

"You are not a natural child of this family," was the stirring and disturbing thought which haunted him throughout his childhood. Simon repeatedly asked himself, "Am I an alien?"

He often wondered to himself and felt lonely in his heart when imagining that perhaps a beggar on the street was one of his parents. He felt no connection to his family.

One school day as a sixth grader, one of his bullying classmates challenged him with violence and yelled in his face. "You are not the natural child of your family!"

Simon was humiliated and furious and unable to control his emotions. He thrashed with his fists in rage and the bully used a broomstick to fight back. They both wound up in the hospital, bruised and defeated with blood streaming down their faces.

When he heard his father's request to the doctor: "Don't give him anesthetic. Suture the wounds directly," Simon was shocked. He couldn't believe what he was hearing. For he didn't know, at that time, that the incident had hurt his father more than his own physical pain.

Simon received seventeen stitches and was dizzy with pain. He was so unseeing and impetuous as a teenager that he failed to notice the fact that his adoptive parents had spent all their savings on him. They treated him as their own and only son.

After Simon graduated from junior high school, he wanted to join the military to become a pilot but this was strictly forbidden by his father, as his father didn't want him to discover the truth that he had been adopted. You have to submit a birth certificate to join the army and they tried to conceal the truth.

However, Simon was eager to know his true origins and was so totally misguided in his heart that he could not feel the love of his adoptive family at all.

Until 1975, he served in the military on the island of White Sands in Penghu, far away from his hometown. He received letters from his father which often counseled him in the simple facts of life, "Be aware of the changing weather." "Put on more clothes to avoid catching colds."

However, there were four sentences from his father which would become his lifetime motto. **"Restrain your impulse to anger. Guard against incautious words and actions. Be alert to errors made in reckless haste. Cherish your hard-earned money."**

From the moment he read those words, Simon understood his father's intentions and thereafter never spoke against his father. He realized how much his father cared for him. He burst into tears and cried out loud and for the first time started to feel a connection and belongingness to his adoptive family.

Years later, the long-awaited day finally arrived when he would finally meet his biological family. At the age of 26, he met his biological brothers, sisters and father for the first time. His feelings about his natural family were confused and complicated. His biological father told him, "Put aside the ones who gave birth to you for those who raised you. They are the ones you should truly pay respect and be grateful to. Don't forget where your livelihood came from."

This understanding directed his future life. He chose to come back to Taiwan and keep company with and take care of his adoptive parents until the end of their lives. He decided he would rather abandon his promising career in the US than to abandon his true family when they needed him most and considered it a gift and blessing from God.

Eventually, Simon became a trained and capable expert in many fields. What runs in his blood is "industriousness." He entered the insurance industry in 1989 and has served his customers with integrity, professionalism and assistance to society. He has never betrayed his commitments in over 25 years of service. That's why his organization "Tien-Cheng Branch of Nan Shan Life Insurance Company" grows larger and larger. Besides insurance, Simon is very active in social networking. He is the leader of numerous communities and organizations including the Business Management Consultants Association of the Republic of China where he trained to be an International Certified Management Consultant and where he currently serves as Vice-Chairman and Executive Director.

He was also hired as the Consultant in Finance of National Policy Foundation and continues to serve in the position to this day.

In Myanmar, he attended the Asia Pacific Annual Conference on behalf of the Business Management Consultants Association and he is constantly trying to introduce and increase cooperation between industry elites from all over the world. Through his many years of service and self-development he has visited many countries and seen many different walks of lives. He is active in social networking and aggressive in learning, often sharing his knowledge and wisdom through lecturing. He has given speeches on diverse topics such as career planning, goal management, marketing, social insurance, practical insurance, financial planning, etc.

One of his guiding principles is that one's life must matter and to not live a vain or wasteful life. He dedicates himself to providing guidance and helping the younger generations. The people who have benefitted from his giving are as many as the stars.

Simon's eyelids become tired but his heart is always burning with great enthusiasm. He is humble but passionate and passes on his love and responsibility to everyone in his life with all his heart.

He is a generous sage who is grateful for all his blessings and never stops passing on the blessing to others.

Starting Over from the Beginning
The Quality Gourmet Food
Su-Ling Kuo（郭素玲）

Dropping the pen and lifting the sword to go into battle is like starting over from a sketch then growing and growing.

On September 31st 2014, the author came to give a speech in Taoyuan, Taiwan. Among the attendees was a tall, slender, decent-looking young woman handing me a business card with both hands- "Delicious Healthy Vegetarian Foods." I liked that card because I have been a vegetarian for over two decades.

Whenever I know there are people making vegetarian food, I feel deeply moved because I realize there is no greater revolutionary fighter than the one who wishes to save the Earth through vegetarian ecology. I especially appreciate anyone who is in the vegetarian food business. Especially in this environment full of food safety issues along with fake vegetarian food products appearing on and off. With dedicated effort, we vegetarians can have secure food options on the market. Otherwise, a healthy and long life for vegetarians is just a false image of an otherwise worthy concept.

I looked closely at this person in front of me and was inspired. She was a shy and reserved girl dressed in a plain outfit. Her smiling eyes showed strong willpower gained from her so-called plain experiences.

To prove females have the ability to protect their own country and to train their own minds and spirit, Su-Ling served in the army for eleven years to become a modern "Hua Mulan". In April 2013 she retired from service as her youthfulness quietly faded.

Released from the uniformity of military service, Su-Ling looked to the sky and searched for a path to her future.

One day while visiting a vegetarian diner run by a friend, she was amazed to discover that a meal without meat could taste so delicious. Su-Ling and one of her friends were inspired to cooperate and develop an entirely new business together.

They started by packaging fresh, steaming hot vegetarian meals into instant frozen food packs and marketing it on the internet. Heating the packs by any method produced delicious edible meat-free meals. This really was good news for vegetarians.

However, ideas remain ideas without practice and Su-Ling and her friend encountered an unexpected "enemy" they had never faced before and they were lacking the tactics to defeat it. The "enemy" consisted of the many legal and business matters such as trademark registration, website establishment, promotional design, hygiene regulations, taxation accounting; none of which Su-Ling understood at all. Nevertheless, she refused to be defeated. Her military training had prepared her to face and overcome her enemies and so, although unexpected, she confronted her foes and developed her strategy to surmount them. The spirit of never surrender had fired her up to bust through the difficulties. Su-Ling believes those experiences were a test of her humanity and not only did they awaken her potential, but also at that moment her endurance was jacked up.

Step by step Su-Ling succeeded and their web store "Top Delicious Healthy Vegetarian Food" was set up and operating within only a few months. This seemed to prove the old military saying: There will be no amateurs after three months of training.

Upon retiring from military duty, Su-Ling understood that everything had to start from scratch. In the real world people don't judge you by your rank or title, but by your capabilities. All sorts of professional strengths are developed through trial and error and she knows real learning is the best way to minimize mistakes. Su-Ling took on a variety of classes to expand her wisdom and to upgrade her own thinking and behavior patterns. Moreover, she participated in business referral groups to transform her marketing strategies from a one-man battle to a campaign of teamwork and cooperation.

After a year of hard work Su-Ling's food team has become so popular that orders from the internet and from referrals have become so abundant, they can scarcely handle them all. Su-Ling has never stopped being grateful for all the training she has had and for all the teachers and mentors who have helped her on her way.

And most of all Su-Ling is grateful to her parents. On November 22nd 2014, she and her family finally gathered together. Su-Ling broke the ice by kissing her mom and dad dearly. That was the first time Su-Ling had shown feelings of tenderness and gratitude to her family. "I love you, mom and dad" That sentiment was more meaningful than anything else she could have said.

Gratitude is continuously reserved.

Bravery is militarily inspired.

Learning is forwardly motivated.

Teamwork is the shortcut to success.

Thus it is said, "Transformation comes from gratitude and bravery brings people together. Starting over from the beginning and refusing to return to zero again."

The Blueprint in My Heart
Passionate Interior Designer
Chung-Yi (Doris) Chen（陳中儀）

I believe any profession can be disciplined. But who believes the ultimate profession in spirits can be disciplined, too?

Doris (Chung-Yi) is a girl who has loved to scribble since she was little. As long as there was a blank spot around, she'd fill it with her scribbles. According to Asian culture, girls should act with a little more reservation. But Doris never left a blank piece of paper around, wherever she lived or stayed.

And although she had won many awards in art, she knew she still had so much room for improvement. In the old and conservative age of Taiwan, very few parents would invest in and cultivate their children who showed a gift or a talent in art. Indeed, it was such an unattainable dream for a little girl to learn from a master of art and to pursue greatness in it.

In her second year of junior high school, Doris set a goal to become an interior designer. It seemed that she was meant to be one. But there was something missing—standardized professional training as well as a cutting-edge means to design.

Doris is grateful to her mentors, Ms. Shu-Ling Chang and Mr. Zheng-Yi Tsai. Both led her as an innocent youngster to the palace levels of art step by step. In 1993 Doris graduated from the National Art Institute of Taiwan and started working in a design firm.

In 1995, she was dispatched to Yantai, Shandong, China where she suddenly expanded her horizons and experienced rapid personal growth. The job overseas proved that traveling to new places provides more experience than merely burying oneself in books. She loved traveling so much; it generated so much creativity and insight in her work.

In 1999, Doris came back to Taiwan to found her own studio in interior design. Since then, improving other designers' professional proficiency and style has been her goal. She wanted to transfigure the inferior stereotypes of this industry in the minds of the general population. Doris came up with a term "Designers' Morality." She hopes all designers will follow their own moral standards in business.

To close a deal and to make a profit are not where Doris puts emphasis in doing business. She has always viewed her clients' cases like designing her own home. She wishes to save clients' money by paying attention to every detail in design -- things her clients wouldn't usually notice or pay attention to. She understands that no-one wants the trouble of frequently redecorating and refurbishing, deriving from a bad original design.

Doris does not usually draw digital 3D layouts. 3D drawing software technology certainly delivers attractive images to consumers; however Doris wants to avoid the disappointment of her customers when they discover the results aren't exactly as the digital drawings show. Instead she puts all of her effort into providing expertly-planned and tailored designs and preventing her customers from being "impulsive when viewing the layouts and heartbroken when seeing the results"

Therefore, Doris has maintained a record of "zero complaints" from her customers. By the end of their relationship each customer has become a friend. With just one phone call, she will help without question and with immediate action, any task from repairing toilets to flower arrangements. Frankly speaking, such an attentive designer is a rare find. Doris says: "This is what a lifetime warranty means!"

The author once asked Doris, "What is your favorite style in design?"

Most designers would like to convince their clients from their own points of view. They design what they like, rather than what their clients prefer. However, Doris replied, "Personally I like American Classics the most, but I rarely advise so. What my clients want is, above all, for me to listen to their thoughts and analyze the pros and cons. I advise professionally and discuss with my clients about the "blueprint in their hearts." Thus, the outcome perfectly meets my standard of Designers' Morality.

Doris finds pleasure in being able to provide her services and receive satisfaction and acknowledgment from customers. For Doris is highly interested in the possibilities of creating and in receiving satisfaction for her designs. Doris remarks, **"Now everything I do is my mission. I'll draw with my humble pen forever, until God requests me to design the blueprint for heaven!**

Hence it is said, **there is no void as long as the emptiness is drawn, even as there are no broken hearts nor shattered dreams. I hold in my mind that the clients' desires are realized in order to create their dream home."**

Born to be a Star
Prince of Lungyen
Jun-Han Chen（陳軍寒）

Nature, science, literature, reading, guitar, bands, singing, sports and working out, these are all interests of the sunny boy, Jun-Han Chen.

His interests are so broad that no-one could associate them with his current job. After graduating from National Taiwan Normal University, he went for his master's degree in Performing Arts.

Subsequently, he taught biology at a cram school for five years. At the same time, he performed in the theatre, in commercials and on TV. He applied what he had learned and although he had a passion for the performing arts, he thought differently than others.

After an inexplicable series of circumstances, he entered the funeral and internment industry. He transformed himself from a performer on stage and screen to a "facilitator of earthly departure." Maybe it could be expressed as a transformation, a theater of a different form. If you search "Jun-Han Chen" on the internet, your attention would linger as the Commercial Film calls, "Listen to the wind in summer."

It goes like this: The girl says, "Make a wish in your mind then shout it out loudly three times. Our ancestors will hear you and realize your wish for you." The girl describes the story of the "rainbow bridge"......

The boy holds the girl's hands and asks her to close her eyes to smell the fragrance from the leaves, the soil and the wind. He says, "Though we cannot capture the wind, we can both feel it. Though we might not be able to come back again, I will always remember the summer when we are here listening to the sound of the wind."

What a beautiful story! Maybe it was the potency of this kind of consideration and spirit that led Jun-Han to wish for the dead to be allowed to have unrepentant souls; but at the same time leave beautiful memories.

Jun Han was born with an outstanding appearance and his deep pupils attracted the pulse of the dead. During a funeral of his relatives, he gained inspiration and insight about the unpredictability of life. He could choose to lecture on stage and capture the hearts of young students and direct them toward diligent learning or he could choose to perform on stage and so capture the admiration of fans and lead them to the boundaries of performing arts.

Jun-Han chose to decline the center stage and instead, to assist in bringing to people the touching and inspirational feelings of a funeral service. He gives all his elegance to the undecayed body and takes the grief and gratitude of the relatives for the dead.

This is selfless assistance, but a worthy achievement. Jun-Han forgets about his fear and the old taboos when facing death. All he considers is respect and value to the deceased. He believes a person doesn't live in vain. For he knows you can't bring anything with you when death arrives, all you possess is Karma. No matter how handsome he looks, he will lose his appearance one day.

Jun-Han chooses to devote himself to providing help whenever he can, rather than indulge in his own appearance; and lead his own dignified team members to provide and prepare the best funeral arrangements.

No one can tell how long you will live and that life is not permanent. Don't regret when death knocks on your door. Be ready and arrange everything in advance. Now the story has played out.

Jun-Han's story reminded the author of a song he wrote for his students at the cram school in Tamsui when he was studying for his Master's Degree in Chemistry at Tamkang University.

"The end of the sunset."

Watching the days goes by. Are you clear about what you're going to accomplish today?

Do you know there is sunset in Tamsui? Do you know what's behind the sunset?

Life is a show, but how many years do you think you can fool around?

Use your youth, don't wait until your hair turns white.

Looking at the light of Guanyin Mountain, we ponder how much time we have to linger.

But don't wait until death strikes to realize you have nothing left. Nothing left.

Innocuous Ecological Angel
Chin-Miao Lai（賴金妙）

An innocuous ecological angel, Chin-Miao speaks with wisdom and love.

Chin-Miao has a pretty appearance but has a boy's disposition due to the boyish environment in which she grew up among many brothers. Chin-Miao has an heroic spirit as well as a strong sense of justice, inculcated by her father.

Since the time she was a second grader, she hasn't had close connection with her family. Both her parents died of heart disease when she was young and genetic heart failure has taken quite a few lives in her family, so naturally Chin-Miao was at risk.

Life is so fragile that we often don't have to wait until we're old to feel like a candle in the wind. Chin-Miao knows well about the uncertainty of human life and so decided to devote herself to a career in medicine as a nurse.

Right after graduating from high school she started working in the ICU (Intensive Care Unit) without hesitation. She has seen many patients linger between the realms of life and death.

In such a circumstance, to die well is a blessing but to die terribly

with agony and struggle could be the worst and cruelest fates on Earth.

Once there was an elderly man in the terminal stages of cancer at ICU. He begged the nurses and doctors with tired eyes and weak voice, "Please stop trying to save me. Do not waste any more of my family's money. I know I can no longer survive. My father and grandfather are here to take me. I'm exhausted! My physical body is done for. Let me go. Continuing the treatment is torture for all of us. So please, please allow me the dignity to decide my own future."

The scenes of farewell tell the truth of the struggle by severely ill patients. Many of them could not control their bodies or their minds and only wished to be able to die with dignity. At a moment like that, to die well is a comfort.

Patients with acute injuries require fast medical attention whereas patients with chronic conditions require more time, costing much more money. Our medical system is able to save the emergency cases; however, is there any mechanism to treat the protracted cases without it costing us so much?

And the ultimate question is, where do many of these chronic diseases stem from? One known cause is the unethical practices in the production of food and corrupt corporations which spread toxins and pollution in the environment for their own selfish profits.

Their effects have insidiously influenced many aspects of our daily lives. The mainstream press are themselves guilty by their indifference since they are often funded by these same corporations through the advertising dollar and serve only to spread more fear, helplessness and propaganda or fail to provide meaningful and constructive coverage. Government law enforcement acts mainly for show while quietly allowing crimes to go unpunished, or be punished too lightly and as time goes by; food crimes and pollution continue to increase.

These many drawbacks have developed into a worldwide dilemma of not knowing what is safe or unsafe to eat or use; the immediate plight which our world is now facing.

Chin-Miao has determined to actively promote the consumption of innocuous and healthy foods as a precaution to achieving health and longevity. These precautions are made to avoid unnecessary medical treatments and to promote a detoxified lifestyle that is environmentally friendly and healthy for body and mind. Thus, Chin-Miao joined with a biotechnology company and is taking the path of an innocuous ecological mission.

There's one thing Chin-Miao knows very well: If she were the only person not littering the Earth, it would never become a cleaner place to live; and if she were the only person doing good deeds the world would still be full of bad intentioned people.

For these and other reasons, Chin-Miao started to cooperate with allied organizations to build a "Green Water Drop League," gathering together people with the same desires and vision.

In 2014, Chin-Miao started the "Big Mouth Town", monitoring and filtering honest food providers to make sure they maintain high standards of harmlessness, environmental friendliness and health. At Big Mouth Town, consumers have the opportunity to discover real quality food sources and where they are able to buy quality foods with no worries about toxic additives or growing methods.

Why "Big Mouth?" Because good ideas need to be shared and good products need to be recommended. Therefore, Chin-Miao formed her coalition of human beings committed to saving society, the environment and the Earth itself through accumulating a directory of quality brands, reputable manufacturers and honest producers. The positive consequences are the ones that create the biggest effects of all. This is Big Mouth's goal and objective. The key to Big Mouth is to say good things out loud and with passion.

The ancient scrolls instruct us to show goodwill and mercy and to share what we have with others with joy. Big Mouth is bringing huge business and happiness to angels.

Recently Chin-Miao gave a birth to a baby boy. From her smile we can easily see her pleasure and happiness. Chin-Miao realizes that to allow her son to grow up peacefully is to be herself healthy and so, too, the environment in which they live.

In addition to Chin-Miao's own diligence, honesty and passionate attitude towards her work, her family and her friends she also wishes sincerely that the Gods protect the good deeds their business generates.

She has asked at her temple by drawing lots for their future. And the lot says, **"The Gods deliver goodness in all deeds. All will be peaceful and prosperous. Better to make more effort to make things become smooth, so everyone can be healthy and live a long life."**

Thus it is said, **"An angel welcomes the gift of fortune and good fortune comes to the successful business."**

Award winning
The Architect who gives Life to his Buildings
Yin-Tso Lai（賴盈佐）

My buildings must be alive.

Growing up with Lai, Shun-Pian Architects & Associates in Kaohsiung, Yin-Tso was born to be an architect. He contributes his emotion and special wit to his building designs. Yin-Tso impresses with his flowing renderings and masterpiece designs drawn with his unique passion and style. Yin-Tso has a Master's Degree from the Institute of Architecture National Cheng Kung University. For him, studying sculpture for seven years was like medical school-it has cultivated a doctor in architectural composition. Yin-Tso loves to discuss his blueprints, drawn from scratch, edge to corner, stroke by stroke. Even with the assistance of modern graphic design programs, it still takes a lot of time and effort.

His business card is impressive but being an architect is not a profession that people normally respect in Taiwan. So in order to understand the needs and trends of the building design market, Yin-Tso left his home town to work as an agent for a real estate company doing marketing and consumer behavioral research. For a long time, building owners in Taiwan have focused only on the beauty of interior design and paid little attention to the beauty and harmony of the exterior. On top of that, there has been no comprehensive and integrated planning. For example, if you don't look from above you will miss pollution of the rivers and mountains.

Notice the unsightly arrangement of buildings in many areas of Taiwan, it is unbearable. Speed, low cost, and quality are the three primary requisites when constructing buildings. However during this recent recession, owners and builders have tended to sacrifice quality.

Such a lack of passion, idealism and aesthetic imagination is depressing to Yin-Tso. The point of being an architect is defeated and passion is replaced by frustration. The obligation of an architect is to please the owner, especially in the crowded and limited but expensive spaces of diamond cities like Taipei. Demand is so high; you can even sell an ugly building without effort. In these circumstances, there has been "no really good stuff" around and according to Yin-Tso's observations; really fantastic buildings have only recently started appearing on the market.

Classical and artistic houses stand in great numbers all around Tainan because of the architectural graduates from National Cheng Kung University. With their comprehensive and integrated planning, along with the prioritization of the geographic environment of Taichung's 7th re-planning district, the superior quality of buildings has started to gain favorable comment. They have also started improving other building qualities.

The governors of Kaohsiung, for example, have vision and foresight. They have hired international aesthetic architectural design teams to improve the overall cityscape in order to expand their economies through tourism. The overall level of architecture has improved as a consequence. It is a great pity that this kind of attitude is rarely seen in other areas.

To expand his vision as an architect, Yin-Tso traveled to Europe for two months, He visited many countries scrutinizing various forms, searching for the spirit in the different kinds of architecture. After Europe he went to America and visited the Salk Institute in La Jolla, California designed by world-renowned architect Louis Kahn. There Yin-Tso studied the atrium, taking notice of the bidirectional water collection at the entrance, which freely uses visual effects to make the water seem like it is flowing to the vast and limitless sky! Yin-Tso witnessed the vitality and living energy of construction. He finally rebooted his spirit for architecture, something he had lost for so long.

ZUOVI Architects Officially launched in 2013, Yin-Tso's design team is complete. Their designs include building interiors, industrial spaces and even furniture. Everything can be custom designed from interior to exterior.

To them, construction is an integration and diagnosis of problems and solutions while enhancing property value. Yin-Tso

has combined three fields of professional designers. He and his colleagues are determined to expand their influence to every corner of the world.

From the very first day, Yin-Tso has envisioned himself as a master architect at an international level. They are also aiming to have complete control of their masterpieces from design to construction without intervention. This is what flows in Yin-Tso's blood along with his dream to upgrade the overall attitude of the construction industry in Taiwan. Some day Taiwan can be proud of its buildings. We will no longer need to go abroad to learn and our buildings will inspire foreigners to visit Taiwan as architectural pilgrims. Yin-Tso is only 35 but he expects to witness this glorious vision within his lifetime. He doesn't just want it to happen; he wants to make it happen! He has taken the initiative.

Yin-Tso has become increasingly selective about his assignments, because he cannot abandon his aspirations and every case is part of his reputation. Yin-Tso's team wants to create high quality buildings each with global insight. They never re-use a design because they believe that every building has its own soul and should not be duplicated. When asked which element is the most important in design, Yin-Tso responded, "The elements of safety, practicality, beauty and impact are all indispensable."

"If you consider Feng Shui there are many details to pay attention to. For example, square shapes should be inside the building, not outside. Also, the beauty of each angle should be considered; and human needs noted as well." Actuarial analysis includes budget, materials and structural construction. They want to create a living, breathing, visionary masterpiece of a building.

To Yin-Tso, not only human beings have souls but buildings, too. They have their own beauty-the beauty of architectural concept (the blood), the beauty of construction (the bone), the beauty of materials (the flesh) and the beauty of quality (the skin).

Yin-Tso has devoted his spirit and his life to be a designer of construction beauty. He uses his imagination to sculpture buildings and infuse them with their own spirit and life.

Muse for Realizing Dreams of Self-esteem
Wen-Ju (Julia) Tsai （蔡紋如）

When you first hear of Xihu in Changhua the first image you are most likely to get is of their famous lamb hot pot but it was also the place where the Doctor of Freya Plastic Surgery was born.

Entering medical school requires extraordinary performance and outstanding test scores. As a consequence, many doctors have inflated egos. However, you will never detect such an attitude from Julia (Wen-Ju) at all. Instead, you will sense immediate attachment from the moment you meet, especially when you hear her rural accent and discover her passion for work and her infectious amiability. Julia does not consider herself a good student but attributes her success to her father's foresight and ambition, such as enrolling her in the foremost girl's high school in Taiwan and then helping her pass the most challenging tests to finally enter the Medical Department of Kaohsiung Medical University.

Before her father became a businessman, he was a junior high school English teacher. He was her exclusive tutor from elementary school to high school. Without his coaching and supervision, there wouldn't be a Dr. Tsai today.

Together they both support the building of self-confidence through

Julia's cosmetic "art center" as a team.

Julia's mother is a professional fashion designer. She is well known on Yongkang Street. Humorous, elegant and romantic are all adjectives which can be used to describe this charismatic lady. She especially adores the classical cultures of Europe. During her childhood, Julia spent each summer and winter vacation traveling and exploring the historical sites and scenic spots of the continent. She and her family immersed themselves in the vivid and lively culture of Western Europe. Julia believes that was the best investment her parents could have made for her and her siblings. Such an experience growing up is indeed enviable and you can still observe the influence Europe has had on Julia in her style and personality. At the same time, you can also sense her family's principles of honor, commitment, and integrity.

An injection of botulinum toxin is reminiscent of the Leaning Tower of Pisa. An irrigate of Hyaluronic acid perfusion is like a gush of hope from the River Thames. A feather light touch of energy waves is like the soothing sun by the Champs Elysees. A breast uplift procedure is like scaling the summit of the Matterhorn.

Cosmetic surgery may aid self-confidence, but one's money must be invested cautiously. Julia never encourages her clients to borrow money to do plastic surgery or to use credit cards. She won't agree to the many abuses of plastic surgery. It violates her moral code to borrow huge sums of money simply to improve one's appearance, because of the financial burden in medical expenses one can easily

incur out of vanity. Her medical patients might need the money to
save their lives, but not her beauty clients. Julia wants to avoid the
popular delusion of expending vast sums of money to change one's
appearance. Hurting someone's financial security and emotional
stability is not the purpose of her clinic.

Julia started as an intern at Chang Gung Memorial Hospital, and
then later became a doctor of allergy immunology at National Taiwan
University Hospital. Later, she entered the research field of anti-
aging cosmetics and medicine. Eventually she was practicing in both
hospital and clinical settings. Now she has begun another journey in
her life by opening the Freya Plastic Surgery Clinic with her husband.

Julia never liked the culture of a fast-paced medical system. Such
a system requires you to diagnose hundreds of patients every day.
The only way to avoid long hours waiting for patients is to diagnose
and provide prescriptions like a robot. How can you administer
honest and accurate treatment in such an environment? What
Julia cares about is finding the real cause of an illness or allergy and
recommending effective treatment. If you can accurately locate the
cause, it is far easier to solve the problem. Why do clients feel the urge
to come to her clinic for cosmetic surgery? Julia believes **lack of self-
confidence plays a role. It is this lack of confidence which produces
dissatisfaction with their physical appearance and a desire to
enhance their features. Knowing this, Julia spends most of her time
listening and advising her clients, rather than on diagnosis. She**

has been in the beauty business for five years and in that time she has accumulated over 2,000 clients and made friends with them all. This is a result she never expected or imagined-that it could be so pleasant and amiable to be a doctor. She expects all her clients to have a happy and comforting experience. When they add to their beauty through cosmetic procedures their confidence grows. Therefore, the title of her new book is "Confident Immunology".

When seeing her clients gain confidence Julia discovers her own satisfaction.

When seeing the radiance in her clients' eyes, Julia finds her own value.

From her perspective they are not only clients and patients. Rather they are friends, neighbors and family members. And although Julia is a medical doctor and her clinic is her livelihood, **in her mind, there is only help-not profit.**

In Julia's words, "Cosmetic Surgery is a combination of science and aesthetics, a surgical operation for the purpose of art and beauty." Her husband Dr. Zheng-Yi Lin is also a professional plastic surgeon and is responsible for the operation of Freya Plastic Surgery. Julia is responsible for the aspects of Art & Beauty. Together they cooperate without flaw and in total symmetry.

Julia is a beautiful doctor happily helping others to realize their own beauty and to regain their self-confidence.

Focus and Vision
Specialized Optometrist
Chih-Hong Hsiao（蕭志鴻）

Chopin wrote the first score of a waltz. Within 25 years of composition he completed 36 of themes in total. The most famous one is Waltz in D-flat major, Op. 64, No. 1 (so-called Minute Waltz). The score is light and cheerful like a puppy, so it is also called "Pup Waltz".

In the 500 days of knowing Chih-Hong Hsiao, the author has been tremendously influenced by the joyful power he generates. One must be happy to gain happiness. That's why Chih-Hong chooses to welcome every experience in his life with optimism.

Chih-Hong has read and studied widely including poetry, classical literature, and medicine since he was a young boy. However, the high spirit of obtaining knowledge did not bring him luck at exams and he failed to become a doctor as originally intended.

Nevertheless, as a graduate of Chung-Hsin University, Chih-Hong dedicated himself to learning the business of medicine in order to fulfill his wishes to help people. He focused on his ambition and subsequently became an optometrist.

In the beginning, Chih-Hong thought optometry was as simple as what he had learned in school but as he was confronted by more and more unsolvable cases, Chih-Hong was motivated to expand his knowledge further. His professors thought that solving the problems of optometry were "way too hard" for Chih-Hong. But driven by a sense of responsibility and curiosity, Chih-Hong spent a total of 15 years studying. Finally, he arrived at his greatest conclusion— optometry really was way too hard!

What is the thing way too hard? That is "specialized optometrist lenses prescription".

About 90% of Chih-Hong's clients have optometrical diseases, such as latent or manifest deviation, amblyopia, low vision that is close to blindness, cataract, cataract, iritis, AMD (age-related macular degeneration), RP (Retinitis Pigmentosa). Other diagnoses are also there like prescriptions before or after optometrical disease operations, LASIK, vision fatigue,progressive or recessive lenses, as well as students' vision tests and eye health maintenances. Yes, they are very hard to understand! Needless to mention those so well known nearsighted, farsighted, astigmatism, andpresbyopia.

In fact, all these are not medical studies. They are instead optics under physics. Optics consists of complex mathematics, so Chih-Hong spends calculating difficult math questions every moment of his harder than CPAs. He realizes just if he made a mistake in any questions it will effect the whole body chemistry by the eyes of his clients.

Being an optometrist is the only job Chih-Hong has had since 1987-28 years! The passion he has for his job allows him to gain achievement, fulfillment and dignity. Every time his satisfied clients show their gratitude, Chih-Hong feels so touched he is sometimes moved to tears. It just manifests his very first wish to help people in solving their problems.

Chih-Hong assists doctors with tough issues in circumstances where operations are needless. The art and science of optometry allows patients be able to return to work with healthy eyes and go on with their lives. This is the kindness and brilliance that Chih-Hong has.

Chih-Hong knows the accumulation of optometric knowledge is not an easy thing to achieve and he feels that it is important to pass on this legacy so he has started recruiting apprentices to learn his skills and by opening Chia-yang Optical Clinics, Chih-Hong hopes to spread his ideas of helping people's eyesight with love and science, to the world.

Chih-Hong considers himself to be a person who tries his best to help like a rainbow after the rain that everyone can see. Thus we now have an ode to joy by Chih-Hong, whose life's work is restoring hope and vision to his patients.

The True Essence of Love
Earnestness and Sincerity
Chih-Hang Cheng（鄭至航）

"A long illness makes the patient into a good doctor." This could be the best proverb to describe the founder of iChangeGo, Stark (Chih-Hang) Cheng.

There is a famous modern anonymous poem, the writer of which the author tried every means to identify but failed. However the author appreciates the classical phrase "Butterfly will naturally be attracted to you if there are plenty of blooming flowers."

The "best weapon" to attract someone is to strengthen ourselves and promote our abilities.

This is another story of misfortune coming from a single parent family. Stark was brought up by his father. Happiness and a stable relationship was his unspoken but most desired dream. Because he was not tall, rich or handsome enough to become popular with the girls who cared only for superficial conditions, the most frequent excuse he got from girls who had rejected him was: "You are too good to be my boyfriend."

In order to break this misconception that women only care about a man's appearance, he wanted to prove to them that the charm of men comes from inside and not the outside. Stark received training in eloquence from a famous school. He read many books about gender relationships, interpersonal communication, body and soul and psychology looking for answers. He persisted without fear of rejection and finally won the first "Yes!" from the first girl he truly admired.

However, it didn't take long for this hard-won love to end. It felt like he had received an "order to leave" school notice. No words could describe the pain. He was heartbroken.

He looked at himself in the mirror, asking, "Why? Why? Why?" The water from the showerhead seemed to keep falling on his mind and on the wounds of his broken heart. Time never healed those wounds caused by the rejection he received as a young man.

Stark asked through his tears, "All I want is a companion to have a heart to heart talk with, to comfort each other with our encouragement. I am not looking for a short term relationship or a one-night stand. I will never barter flirtatiously with girls. Why is this so difficult?"

Fortunately, Stark was born with an indomitable spirit. He continued with full effort, over and over to be more forward in the "battlefield of love". Eventually, he learned his most precious lesson and realized that **you don't have to pursue love. Love is attracted to you-although it's still good to proactively manage and plan your**

pursuit for true love. Be an active Crusader.

From this moment on, Stark became a conqueror in his love battle and captured the heart and mind of his true love. He noticed that there were so many men and women, very much in the same boat and suffering like him who were confused and depressed without any solutions.

As a result, Stark founded iChangeGo in 2008. He meant to build a "love bridge" for lonely men and women to cross in order to help them accomplish their goals. It is like a love gospel for males and females. From then on iChangeGo became so well known, he started to publish books and materials to coach people about how to gain love. He was interviewed in the press and gave endless speeches. His foundation became a hope of love for people in despair.

Unfortunately, there were some people with dishonorable intent who only wanted to learn how to get a one night stands or flirting skills with women.

No. Stark insists on his principles, "My foundation is to help you find your true love and to overcome any difficulty. The goal is to lead you to success and to having a happy relationship. It's not a means for you to commit further sins, for I'm not here to teach people to flirt."

Hence it is said: **Create your own value sincerely and show your attractiveness and charm to discover your own happiness.**

Fortune Goddess
Testimonies of Miracle
Su-Yu Chung（鐘絲雨）

Yu-Chen Chung spent two and half years in Japan during elementary school and after she graduated from the Applied Japanese Language Department of Ming Chuan University, she went to Canada to study for her MBA. These environments have led Ssu-Yu to know multiple foreign languages.

Her art-loving parents brought her everywhere on the planet, except Africa. Ssu-Yu has been to more countries than one can imagine.

Ssu-Yu was influenced by Japanese Shinto witchcraft and began practicing Usui Reiki and Longevitology Reiki. She even took internships at Taiwanese temples drawing Taoism magic notes to recover one's soul.

Ssu-Yu's father was Catholic and her mother was a Taoist. Her religious upbringing was without boundaries so she never set limits on her spiritual path.

In October 2007, a car accident happened and the left side of her body was paralyzed. However, an extensive eyesight was opened up by surprise. She then could see many layers of spaces and beings. It was as if you gain something you must lose something as well. Or reversely? Nothing at the moment mattered to her anymore.

Then heaven gave her a new name Ssu-Yu Chung, expecting her to think counterclockwise and never be beaten by fate. She comes forth in a silk like rain without leaving a water mark on her body and soul, which is the most professional spiritual practice.

The arrangement of fate for her has two reasons:

The first is like Mencius said, "When Heaven is about to place a great responsibility on a man, it always first frustrates his spirit and will, exhausts his muscles and bones, exposes him to starvation and poverty, harasses him by troubles and setbacks so as to stimulate his mind, toughen his nature and enhance his abilities."

The other is Karma.

It is either to enhance her abilities or mere Karma. Since then, why bother? Why feel sorry and complain?

After a year of being paralyzed, one of the eye began to degenerate. No doctor could do anything about her eyesight. Through a long term of inner conflicts, it was the power of hypnosis helped her bring back her health. The power of the soul controls everything that works in our body.

Ssu-Yu began to systematically research, learn and integrate spiritual methods and she reads extensively. She is qualified as an international hypnotherapist by the National Guild of Hypnotists, a recognized psychological consultant in China, an executive of NLP recognized by Neuro-Linguistic Programming University, a training teacher of hypnotherapists and a legacy teacher at Yuan-cheng Temple.

In the TV show, Fate Is So Much Fun she has had wonderful performances. Ssu-Yu is grateful for that, but that isn't the direction she wants to go.

She hopes through direct interaction she could offer help to traumatized souls.

Most people consider spiritualism as a mysterious magic. Actually it is the beautiful art of nature. There is no need for modern medicine or medical practices, situational encouragement by scenic atmospheres or empty goal setting slogans. It is merely original spiritual analysis and the blessing of converted universal energy.

Ssu-Yu's career objective is to deliver good effects, to make more friends and pass on happiness.

Thus it is said, **"Once traumatic memories are deleted from your life, one will settle in a house of good fortune. Such a blessing is like a fire to light up way in the drizzling rain."**

Chapter VIII

Glossary

Andrew and Jihong Hall

National director for BNI® in China, Hong Kong, Macau & Taiwan

Cambridge University,Economics, MA

Recognized expert on word of mouth marketing.

Author of the book, The Handy Guide to Networking 2001

Contributing author to World #1 best-selling book, Masters of Success

Acclaimed public speaker, receiving invitations to speak to 1,000s of business professionals in Europe the United States and Asia.

Beth Misner

Co-Founder for BNI® Foundation and Co-Owner for BNI®, the world's largest business networking organization.

Together with her husband, Ivan, she owns and operates both BNI® and the BNI® Foundation. One of the greatest joys of her life is traveling to our BNI® countries and meeting our enthusiastic and supportive members. I also get a thrill out of finding deserving educational programs for kids to which to donate our Givers Gain Grants.The new Business Voices movement is something she is totally passionate about. When business owners fully realize the power we have to positively impact education and the future for at-risk kids, lives will be changed for the good all over the planet!

BNI®

BNI® is the world's largest business networking, referrals and word of mouth marketing organization. This website provides information on BNI® international news, as well as a database of BNI®'s worldwide chapters and listing of Directors, information on how to join and much, much more!

Cao Cao 曹操

(IPA:; 155 – 15 March 220), courtesy name Mengde, was a warlord and the penultimate Chancellor of the Eastern Han dynasty who rose to great power in the final years of the dynasty. As one of the central figures of the Three Kingdoms period, he laid the foundations for what was to become the state of Cao Wei and was posthumously honoured as "Emperor Wu of Wei". Although he is often portrayed as a cruel and merciless tyrant, Cao Cao has also been praised as a brilliant ruler and military genius who treated his subordinates like his family. He was also skilled in poetry and martial arts and wrote many war journals.

Confucius 孔子

The philosophy of Confucius emphasized personal and governmental morality, correctness of social relationships, justice and sincerity. His followers competed successfully with many other schools during the Hundred Schools of Thought era only to be suppressed in favor of the Legalists during the Qin Dynasty. Following the victory of Han over Chu after the collapse of Qin, Confucius's thoughts received official sanction and were further developed into a system known as Confucianism.

Confucius is traditionally credited with having authored or edited many of the Chinese classic texts including all of the Five Classics, but modern scholars are cautious of attributing specific assertions to Confucius himself.Aphorisms concerning his teachings were compiled in the Analects, but only many years after his death.

Confucius's principles had a basis in common Chinese tradition and belief. He championed strong family loyalty, ancestor worship, respect of elders by their children and of husbands by their wives. He also recommended family as a basis for ideal government. He espoused the well-known principle "Do not do to others what you do not want done to yourself", an early version of the Golden Rule.

Da-Shu Wu 吳大樹

Founder of Sea Biscuit club, By My Way Educational institutions, By My Way digital information, The Secretary-General of Chinese Digital Educational Development Association.

He got the educational training for Nirvana Memorial Garden Pte.

Ltd through a phone call by the member of Yung En Chapter, Tang Zheng Xiang, whose profession is in Interior Design. They arranged his traveling and accommodation with the payment of 2000 Ringgit Malaysia (U.S. 650) per hour. He got this referral through word of mouth, without any previous relationship or meeting in advance. That's his ideal referral.

Dong Zhuo 董卓

Dong Zhuo (died 22 May 192),[1] courtesy name Zhongying, was a politician and warlord who lived in the late Eastern Han Dynasty. He seized control of the capital Luoyang in 189 when it was in a state of turmoil following the death of Emperor Ling and a clash between the eunuch faction and some court officials led by General-in-Chief He Jin. Dong Zhuo subsequently deposed Emperor Shao and instated Emperor Xian.

Dong Zhuo rose to power in the Han imperial court and ruled the nation with tyranny and cruelty for a brief period of time. The following year, a coalition of regional officials and warlords launched a punitive campaignagainst Dong, forcing him to move the capital to Chang'an. Dong Zhuo was assassinated in 192 by his foster son Lü Bu as part of a plot orchestrated by Interior Minister Wang Yun.

Givers Gain

The philosophy of this organization is built upon the idea of "Givers Gain®": By giving business to others, you will get business in return. This is predicated on the age-old idea of "What goes around, comes around."

Ivan Misner®

Dr. Ivan Misner® the Founder and Chief Visionary Officer for BNI®, the world's largest business networking organization.

He has been called the "father of modern networking" by CNN and one of the "Top Networking Experts to Watch" by Forbes. He is a New York Times Bestselling author who has written more than 20 books. In addition, he is the Co-Founder of the BNI® Foundation.

Lord Mengchang 孟嘗君

Lord Mengchang born Tian Wen, was an aristocrat of the State of Qi during the Warring States Period of China. He was born as Tian Wen, son of Tian Ying and grandson of King Wei of Qi. He succeeded to his father's fief in Xue. Lord Mengchang is well known for the size of his entourage. According to the Records of the Grand Historian, he had up to three thousand people in his retinue. Lord Mengchang eventually become the Chancellor of Qi and of Wei. He was also one of the Four Lords of the Warring States.

Lu Bu 呂布

Lü Bu (died February 199),courtesy name Fengxian, was a military general and warlord who lived in the late Eastern Han dynasty. Originally a subordinate of a minor warlord Ding Yuan, he betrayed and murdered Ding and defected to Dong Zhuo, the warlord who controlled the Han central government in the early 190s. In 192, he turned against and killed Dong Zhuo after being instigated by Wang Yun and Shisun Rui.

Mencius 孟子

Mencius, also known by his birth name Meng Ke or Ko, was born in the State of Zou, now forming the territory of the county-level city of Zoucheng (originally Zouxian), Shandong province, only thirty kilometres (eighteen miles) south of Qufu, Confucius' birthplace.

He was an itinerant Chinese philosopher and sage, and one of the principal interpreters of Confucianism. Supposedly, he was a pupil of Confucius' grandson, Zisi. Like Confucius, according to legend, he travelled throughout China for forty years to offer advice to rulers for reform.[7] During the Warring States period (403–221 BC), Mencius served as an official and scholar at the Jixia Academy in the State of Qi (1046 BC to 221 BC) from 319 to 312 BC. He expressed his filial devotion when he took three years leave of absence from his official duties for Qi to mourn his mother's death. Disappointed at his failure to effect changes in his contemporary world, he retired from public life.

Norm Dominguez

Norm Dominguez is Vice Chairman Emeritus of BNI®, the world's largest referral marketing organization. His relationship with BNI® spans nearly three decades, having started as a member of a chapter in Scottsdale, Arizona in 1987. Over the years he has served in many BNI® capacities, which include U.S. National Director and CEO. He is partnered in BNI® franchises in the State of Arizona. Happiness and positivity are favorite topics of discussion and he believes that life is remarkable. He is a graduate of the University of Colorado. Norm and his wife Sandi reside in Scottsdale.

Shiji 史記

The Records of the Grand Historian (Chinese: Tàishǐgōng shū 太史公書), now known as the Shǐjì 史記–(Scribe's records), is a monumental history of ancient China and the world finished around 109 BC by the Han dynasty official Sima Qian after having been started by his father, Sima Tan, Grand Astrologer to the imperial court. The work covers the world as it was then known to the Chinese and a 2500-year period from the age of the legendary Yellow Emperor to the reign of Emperor Wu of Han in the author's own time.[1]

The Records has been called a "foundational text in Chinese

civilization."[2] After Confucius and the First Emperor of Qin, "Sima Qian was one of the creators of Imperial China, not least because by providing definitive biographies, he virtually created the two earlier figures."[3] The Records set the model for the 24 subsequent dynastic histories of China. Unlike Western historical works, the Records do not treat history as "a continuous, sweeping narrative", but rather break it up into smaller, overlapping units dealing with famous leaders, individuals, and major topics of significance.

Sims Qian 司馬遷

Sima Qian (pronounced [sɨmd tɕʰjæ̌n]; c. 145 or 135 – 86 BC), formerly romanized Ssu-ma Chien, was a Chinese historian of the Han dynasty. He is considered the father of Chinese historiography for his work, theRecords of the Grand Historian, a Jizhuanti-style (history presented in a series of biographies) general history of China, covering more than two thousand years from the Yellow Emperor to his time, during the reign ofEmperor Wu of Han. Although he worked as the Court Astrologer (Chinese: 太史令; Tàishǐ Lìng), later generations refer to him as the Grand Historian (Chinese: 太史公; Tàishǐ Gōng or tai-shih-kung) for his monumental work; a work which in later generations would often only be somewhat tacitly or glancingly acknowledged as an achievement only made possible by his acceptance and endurance of punitive actions against him, including imprisonment, castration, and subjection to servility.

Stephen Wu 吳政宏

He applies the executive and management skills from L. Ron Hubbard to assist the entrepreneurs in Asia to become champion and business role mode.He solves problem in expansion cultivate management team create value and build system

The Analects of Confucius 論語

The Analects (Chinese: 論語; pinyin: Lúnyǔ; literally: "Edited Conversations"), also known as the Analects of Confucius, is a collection of sayings and ideas attributed to the Chinese philosopher Confucius and his contemporaries, traditionally believed to have been written by Confucius' followers. It is believed to have been written during the Warring States period (475 BC–221 BC), and it achieved its final form during the mid-Han dynasty (206 BC–220 AD). By the early Han dynasty the Analects was considered merely a "commentary" on the Five Classics, but the status of the Analects grew to be one of the central texts of Confucianism by the end of that dynasty. During the late Song dynasty (960-1279) the importance of the Analects as a philosophy work was raised above that of the older Five Classics, and it was recognized as one of the "Four Books". The Analects has been one of the most widely read and studied books in China for the last 2,000 years, and continues to have a substantial influence on Chinese and East Asian thought and values today.

Confucius believed that the welfare of a country depended on the moral cultivation of its people, beginning from the nation's leadership. He believed that individuals could begin to cultivate an all-encompassing sense of virtue through ren, and that the most basic step to cultivating ren was devotion to one's parents and older siblings. He taught that one's individual desires do not need to be suppressed, but that people should be educated to reconcile their desires via rituals and forms of propriety, through which people could demonstrate their respect for others and their responsible roles in society. He taught that a ruler's sense of virtue was his primary prerequisite for leadership. His primary goal in educating his students was to produce ethically well-cultivated men who would carry themselves with gravity, speak correctly, and demonstrate consummate integrity in all things.

Three kingdoms 三國演義

Romance of the Three Kingdoms, attributed to Luo Guanzhong, is a historical novel set in the turbulent years towards the end of the Han dynasty and the Three Kingdoms period in Chinese history, starting in 169 CE and ending with the reunification of the land in 280.

The story – part historical, part legend, and part mythical – romanticises and dramatises the lives of feudal lords and their retainers, who tried to replace the dwindling Han dynasty or restore it. While the novel follows hundreds of characters, the focus is mainly on the three power blocs that emerged from the remnants of the Han dynasty, and would eventually form the three states of Cao Wei, Shu Han, and Eastern Wu. The novel deals with the plots, personal and military battles, intrigues, and struggles of these states to achieve dominance for almost 100 years.

Tom Fleming

BNI® Executive Director in Tampa/West Central Florida

The BNI team in the Tampa, Gainesville, and Ocala area is always focused on the 4 M's of BNI - Members making more money. They do this by partnering with Tampa and Gainesville entrepreneurs and professionals to build networking groups and through educating them on how to use relationship marketing and networking skills to generate referrals.

He specifically enjoys helping financial advisers, insurance agents, realtors, and mortgage originators—they like to call them the FIRM-learn how to make more money in less time while having lots of FUN !

Warring States period 戰國時代

The Warring States period is a period in ancient China following the Spring and Autumn period and concluding with the victory of the state of Qin in 221 BC, creating a unified China under the Qin dynasty. Different scholars use dates for the beginning of the period ranging between 481 BC and 403 BC, but Sima Qian's date of 475 BC is most often cited. Most of this period coincides with the second half of the Eastern Zhou dynasty, although the Chinese sovereign (king of Zhou) was merely a figurehead.

The name of the period was derived from the Record of the Warring States, a work compiled early in the Han dynasty.

Zhuang Zhou 莊子

Zhuang Zhou, often known as Zhuangzi ("Master Zhuang")[1] was an influential Chinese philosopher who lived around the 4th century BC during the Warring States period, a period corresponding to the summit ofChinese philosophy, the Hundred Schools of Thought. He is credited with writing—in part or in whole—a work known by his name, the Zhuangzi, which expresses a philosophy of skepticism, arguing that life is limited and knowledge to be gained is unlimited.

Big in Business 大商的味道

作　　　者／Ivan Misner、Beth Misner、Norm Dominguez、許宏、黃心慧
統 籌 編 輯／莊陽生物科技集團 http://www.hybt.com.tw
　　　　　　法拉儷國際有限公司 http://www.mireya.com.tw
　　　　　　新北市中和區中山路二段389號6樓
　　　　　　電話：(02)2223-8918 傳真：(02)2223-9339
英 文 編 輯／天下英文
　　　　　　台北市大安區敦化南路一段205號16樓1606室
　　　　　　電話：(02)7713-9858
封 面 設 計／賴盈佐(佐為建築師事務所/佐為國際有限公司)
中 文 校 稿／簡菱瑤、林儷、劉秀霞、黃洛妤
英 文 校 稿／Ronald Y Chen、Ian Jason Cairns, 高瑾彤、范育誠、蕭禎
美 術 編 輯／申朗創意

總 　 編 　 輯／賈俊國
副 總 編 輯／蘇士尹
行 銷 企 畫／張莉滎‧廖可筠

發 　 行 　 人／何飛鵬
出 　 　 　 版／布克文化出版事業部
　　　　　　台北市中山區民生東路二段141號8樓
　　　　　　電話：(02)2500-7008 傳真：(02)2502-7676
　　　　　　Email：sbooker.service@cite.com.tw
發 　 　 　 行／英屬蓋曼群島商家庭傳媒股份有限公司城邦分公司
　　　　　　台北市中山區民生東路二段141號2樓
　　　　　　書虫客服服務專線：(02)2500-7718；2500-7719
　　　　　　24小時傳真專線：(02)2500-1990；2500-1991
　　　　　　劃撥帳號：19863813；戶名：書虫股份有限公司
　　　　　　讀者服務信箱：service@readingclub.com.tw
香港發行所／城邦(香港)出版集團有限公司
　　　　　／香港灣仔駱克道193號東超商業中心1樓
　　　　　　電話：+852-2508-6231 傳真：+852-2578-9337
　　　　　　Email：hkcite@biznetvigator.com
馬新發行所　城邦(馬新)出版集團 Cité (M) Sdn. Bhd.
　　　　　　41, Jalan Radin Anum, Bandar Baru Sri Petaling,
　　　　　　57000 Kuala Lumpur, Malaysia
　　　　　　電話：+603- 9057-8822 傳真：+603- 9057-6622
　　　　　　Email：cite@cite.com.my
印 　 　 刷　卡樂彩色製版印刷有限公司
初 　 　 版　2015年(民104)08月
售 　 　 價　420元

城邦讀書花園　布克文化
www.cite.com.tw　www.sbooker.com.tw

Big in Business

Author： Ivan Misner / Beth Misner / Norm Dominguez / Hsu, Hung / Huang, Hsing-Hui

Overall Editor： Hung Young Bio-tech Group http://www.hybt.com.tw
FALALEY International Ltd http://www.mireya.com.tw/
6F., No.389, Sec. 2, Zhongshan Rd., Zhonghe Dist.,
New Taipei City 23558, Taiwan (R.O.C.)
Tel: 886-2-22238918 Fax: 886-2-22239339

English Editor： World English http://www.travish.com.tw
Rm. 1606, 16F., No.205, Sec. 1, Dunhua S. Rd., Da'an Dist.,
Taipei City 106, Taiwan (R.O.C.)
Tel: 886-2-77139858
Cover Design： Yin-Tso Lai (ZUOVI Architects)
Chinese Proofreading： Chien, Ling-Yao/ Lin, Li/ Liu, Hsiu-Hsia/ Huang, Lo-Yu
English Translation： Huang, Hsing-Hui/ Louise Xiao
English：Proofreading： Ronald Y Chen/Ian Jason Cairns/ Kao, Chin-Tung/ Pai, Tzu-Yu
Art Editor： Chu, Yu-Hsuan

Editor in Chief： Chia, Chun-Kuo
Deputy Editor： Su, Shih-Yin
Marketing Planning： Chang, Li-Hsing/ Liao, Ko-Yun

Publisher / Ho, Fei-Peng
Published / SBOOKER PUBLICATIONS
8F., No.141, Sec. 2, Minsheng E. Rd., Zhongshan Dist.,
Taipei City 104, Taiwan (R.O.C.)
Tel: 886-2-25007008 Fax: 886-2-25027676
Email sbooker.service@cite.com.tw
Issued / Cité Media Holding Group
2F., No.141, Sec. 2, Minsheng E. Rd., Zhongshan Dist.,
Taipei City 104, Taiwan (R.O.C.)
Customer Service line: 886-2-25007718; 886-2-25007719
24 hours Fax: 886-2-25001990; 886-2-25001991
Postal Transfer Acct: 19863813 (BOOKWORM CLUB CO., LTD.)
Service Email: service@readingclub.com.tw
Hong Kong published / Cité Media Holding Group(Hong Kong)
193 Lockhart Road, Wanchai, Hong Kong (Tung Chiu Commercial Centre 1F)
Tel: +852-2508-6231 Fax: +852-2578-9337
Email: hkcite@biznetvigator.com
Malaysia published / Cité (M) Sdn Bhd.
41, Jalan Radin Anum, Bandar Baru Sri Petaling,
57000 Kuala Lumpur, Malaysia
Tel: +603-9057-8822 Fax: +603-9057-6622
Email: cite@cite.com.my
Print / Color Printing
First Published / 2015.08
Selling Price / NT$420

城邦讀書花園　布克文化
www.cite.com.tw　WWW.SBOOKER.COM.TW